"Let Go"

Chapter Twelve

Chapter Twelve

Excerpt from the book, "Imagine…What's Inside"

by Kyleellen

Dedication

"Imagination is more important than knowledge." Albert Einstein

Thanks to Christian and dedicated to Lauren Stalnecker for his "Vision" and to the Brave

Walking Wounded.

If once in my life I could stand up for anything; I'd like to say I stood up to sing.

Imagine….What's Inside?

Ellen St. Peter

The Book about Ln—Come on and Sing

Artwork Roger Ingalls

Copyrights © 2004

All Rights Reserved

ISBN

Disclaimer

Preface

This is how to enjoy the experience of reading my book:

My intentions while writing were always focused on helping others to navigate their own lives. It is my hope that while reading, you take the time to reminisce about your own life's journey and what part your creative mind has played. At the end of each chapter are ideas for each person to think about and perhaps grow from, too.

This book shows how I finally expressed the blessings of my musical ability in a deep, meaningful way and the journey that took me there. It is a book to show one creative, musical person's struggles and triumphs. It allows the reader to see the path I strayed from and came back to as a musical, creative person and what helped me to arrive to the finish line with pride and dignity. I expressed my talent in a positive and fulfilling way. I wrote this book as a documentary to allow people to see what it feels to be different while growing up with a creative talent. Any strong talent always keeps you searching to find where that talent belongs.

I used discretion to decide which events in my life to write about. When I have decided to discuss something, it is done from my point of view in an honest and open way. I have kept a couple of dark skeletons to myself after talking in the privacy of counseling with Dr. Rubel, a supportive professional.

This book is a demonstration of perseverance, which we all must remember to hold onto. It speaks to the reader about being creative in a positive way instead of going in a negative direction. Hopefully it will make you reflect about your own life's journey and in the end leave you wanting to live at your life in a more creative manner. It is a book to show you how you can become less inhibited to

sing and be more creative in your own life, everyday. Enjoy!

Nothing makes me feel better than singing—whether I'm happy or sad, alone or with people. My singing voice has been my best friend all my life. It was always there and free to play with, which probably explains why, as an infant, my mother would tell my older brother to rock my cradle when I was fussing. But, as my brother has remarked, "You weren't truly fussing, you were just making a noise." I was already experimenting with my voice!

What else in life is neither illegal, immoral, nor fattening, but rather is healthy and free? (That is, unless you walk into a recording studio.) Singing is a natural process; our bodies are designed by God to sing, so WHY ARE YOU SHY OF SINGING?

So why are most of us shy to sing? I began pondering this question in college and it lead me on an adventure as I, myself, learned how to stand up and sing (as I'm addicted to singing), and it feels great! I love it and truly feel that God has blessed me with the ability to do this one thing better than anything else. Unfortunately, life events have molded me into one of the most inhibited and phobic closet singers in the world. This is the story of how that huge fear evolved—what I learned about the healing effects of music and singing, and how I overcame a deathly fear of using my natural wide vocal range to perform openly around people. It's also a book about what I learned from the music business and recording in studios, which at times has been brutal psychologically, physically and emotionally. It's a book that I hope will show others the path to enjoying singing for what it truly should be: a fun, free, playful, stress relieving, oxygen-increasing activity. Everyone (and I mean everyone!) is capable of doing this for better health and overall well-being in life.

The trick is to be completely free of all inhibitions and negatively judging—to performing vocally to the best of your capabilities. Not everyone will be an Olympic runner, but most of us learn to run at a young age. Likewise, most of us have learned to sing at a young age, but just because America Idol" may not be in the cards doesn't mean this activity should be forgotten, because singing has tremendous health benefits physically, emotionally, psychologically, and spiritually.

Singing is my life. It's me at my deepest place and it has been for as long as I can remember. My mother claims I was singing by the age of two years, but my first memory is at three, playing on the floor next to my older brother Toad. He was instructing me on which harmony part to sing. He had me singing the low melody, while he sang the middle notes and my only sister (three years older) sang the high notes. It's a clear memory.

I want you to think now of the first time you sang, or the first time you remember singing.

I fell in love with singing from the start. To me it feels like pure Gold is raining down, bathing over my entire body. There's a feeling of heaven on earth or being mesmerized like cheddar colored cats after playing with catnip. The best part is, singing is FREE! The best things in life are free, as the saying goes, so why are so many people in society passing it up? If anyone of any age, gender, nationality or location in the world can sing for free in most places without bothering others, my question is this: why are most people not singing freely? Like I was, they are hiding when they sing. And it's no wonder. For example: why, if I'm walking around and singing, do strangers look at me like I'm crazy or doing something strange? All I'm doing is singing, not committing a crime.

I haven't just escaped from the insane asylum!

Here is the start of the odyssey of a talented and vocally gifted child. The odyssey of Ellen.

If baring my soul helps one child experience his or her own musical odyssey easier, or helps one parent of a creative child (whether in music, art, dance, acting etc.) understand that this talent is not a choice, then I am willing and gladly ready to finally expose my musical odyssey with all its pain and happiness to the world. I hope to help these parents realize that it's not easy to be blessed by God with creative talent. After all, it is we as a society who benefit from the works of positive creative thinking people. Even though art is in the eye of the beholder, the world would be a sad and boring place without the creative arts. Just as in the movie Apollo 13 in which the astronauts were saved by the creative thinking minds of dedicated, hardworking ground support people who didn't give up to create the right solution to a potentially tragic situation, most of the solutions to today's problems will come from a creative mind and spirit.

In reading this book you will learn about:

1) Singing freely for mental, physical, emotional, and spiritual health.

2) Positive creation for happiness in life rather than creating negative behaviors.

3) How to get past and regain your creative spirit when someone hurts or steals your creative work or ideas.

Working on hope can build a bridge and faith will make it a strong one to last a lifetime. Meeting Spiritual musical family. What a Christian can do for you. Fairy God Mothers. The Blessing of giving of yourself to help others. How singing music is my gift to my world, God and myself. Back to the farm and your roots. What's life all about people who care. Lauren's tremendous positive influence. When a producer finally gets it ⍰ My friendly muse for the book. The power of the girl thing supporting you on to your future sharing girl talk with a great young woman and singer Candace. The fulfillment of a promise to myself made when five-years-old the first night after being sexually abused to follow my rainbow until the dream of having a record of me singing was a reality. Thank God Let Go Amen.

For several days, I looked at and even picked up the business card given to me by the stranger, Lauren Stalnecker. His card said, "Lauren Vision, Lauren International, Inc. Producer, Melrose Ave, and Los Angeles." After I picked up and read the card several times, I would then set it down with hesitation. I pondered the million-dollar question: Was this man Lauren another nightmare and dead end, or could he possibly be the right choice for me to call? I placed the card slowly onto my computer keyboard and stared out the bedroom window, afraid of the possibility that this call would lead me to the wrong place; but I wondered if this was the right one. I only know there was never a time of deciding against this, except once, when I held the card over the trash can. I just could not let go of this business card with the word "Vision" and one eye drawn on it.

I'd had a vision late at night after being sexually abused where I undoubtedly knew that God had blessed me to be an exceptional singer and that someday that voice singing would be recorded and played worldwide. I was in awe as a small child as the vision became stronger. I sensed this from outside of me. Soon, a peaceful sensation was covering my wounded soul from the knowledge that something loved me completely.

Vision; the word echoed in my mind while I laid the card I had just saved from the trash back down on my keyboard. I was trying hard to make a conscious and smart decision, yet I felt almost too tired to go any further with singing. Hopelessness crept into my heart until the tears fell, and then that was it. I decided it was better to at least call than to give up. I figured if this man was another evil musical person, the risk had to be taken, because maybe he was true and he was the opposite: a good guy. Maybe this time, "happily ever after" would come, and my voice would find its proper place where people would be able to hear my singing. I hoped to raise money for charities that would benefit people; to give back to the walking wounded in thanks for God blessing me with my voice and everything else I have gratefully received in my life. I don't need the money, or fame, but I do need to sing or I will bust with deep inner pain.

Dialing the number on the card was easy. I felt assertive, for better or for worse, with my singing and myself. I prayed for God's help and protection, and the phone rang as my heart was still. I held my breath, and then the message machine played on the other end. I had mixed emotions. I pondered quickly whether or not I should hang up. I reflected on the prior brief phone conversation with Rue. She had encouraged me to call to at least check out what this Lauren producer was about. Rue said, "Calling and talking to this man doesn't mean you will take the next step and work with him. Just see what he says to you about music and producing. Maybe this guy is an honest music producer."

On his answering machine, I left a brief message and my phone number. I had been standing up nervously to make the call and now sat back down at the computer. I was relieved to be off the fence and headed in some direction. No matter what was to come of this, I felt better than the numerous days of indecisiveness. Again, the music ship set sail and I prayed I was on the right course. It was December 26th, 2003, at 4:30 p.m.

I sat working at my computer with slight anxiety as to when Mr. Lauren Stalnecker would be calling back. I would give him a week but not a month to respond. Twenty minutes went by as I worked on the computer when the phone rang. I answered the phone, convinced it was safe because it was not likely to be Lauren calling so soon. Boy was I wrong. I was alarmed to hear his vaguely familiar voice politely announcing who he was and asking to speak to Ellen. Whoa! My mind switched into business gear and I quickly stood up to get focused. Nervously pacing the floor, I accepted the call and identified myself. Soon these formalities were over and I calmly spoke my mind. I questioned him with my business negotiating skills that I learned from interactions growing up with my father. I asked him things while taking in his answers. I thought about how this unknown stranger, Lauren, had intrigued me so much as to not have thrown his card away. I glanced at the trash can by the desk and then his business card clasped in my hand. I looked at his name on the card as he spoke confidently and professionally about the business of music. Before we hung up, I gave him the house phone number and we had settled upon my thinking about meeting him to discuss his producing music for me.

After hanging up the phone, I sat down in shock. I had the overwhelming feeling, "Here I go again: the music ball is rolling and it feels rather fast." I prayed for God's protection, guidance, and mercy. All I want to do is sing—not be skinned alive, just sing. It was too hard to believe that maybe this time, the business end of my music would work out. I screamed inside, wondering why I, born into a family of everything except professional musicians, was to figure my way through this complex music business. It felt like it was a huge labyrinth full of dead ends and harsh traps, but somewhere the glorious finish line existed. Only where? Would this producer Lauren help me to get there? Only God would know and God would be with me wherever this turn of events was to flow.

Two days later, on December 28th, I called and left a brief message for Mr. Stalnecker to call me when possible. All I wanted to know was the bottom line of how much money he wanted to create the music tracks and record my singing vocals. Rue and Laura had encouraged me to call him and cut to the chase by finding out if the money he would be asking for was within reason or not. I had begun to write down a list of questions to ask him. When Mr. Stalnecker called, he first apologized for the lapse in hours responding to me, as he had been working with someone in the studio. The second thing he insisted was to please call him "Lauren," and that he felt more comfortable with that than the formal "Mr. Stalnecker."

I agreed and offered for him to call me Ellen, or L. Again, I approached him about recording and not wanting to waste his time or mine. I asked for the ballpark figure of the money he would expect to be paid. For a moment, he skirted around the issue with talk of it depending on the instrumentation and other technical aspects of the recording business that I wanted. He tried his hardest to get me to come speak face-to-face with him. I was not ready for that without having more time to think about what the goals were and to gather my strength to deal with another person on the business end of music. I almost felt sorry for Lauren, because he had no idea how leery of musicians and the music business I was. He was going to have to deal with me on my terms and my terms only. He finally understood about giving me a ballpark price of what complete mastered recordings with my vocals perfect (in my opinion) with everything needed would be. I told him that I wanted to be able to think it over before coming to see him. Finally I said, "If you can't tell me, we can't do business."

My heart sank wondering, "How did that come out of me?" I was scared to death to hear his response, thinking for sure he would end the conversation. Instead, he understood me clearly, telling me the price today would be about sixteen to seventeen hundred dollars per track, and that he could be a little flexible depending upon what all would be included in the finished song. Again he humbly asked to see me in person today. I spoke up quickly saying, "Not today. It's my wedding anniversary."

He didn't know, but my anniversary gift for myself was calling him and praying this day would bring me good luck dealing on the phone with a producer of music. He suggested that we have a meeting tomorrow or sometime before the first of the year. I thought, "He's a nut! It's holiday time and I have two children at home!" Eventually he understood, ending the conversation with, "Please do call to set up a time to meet and let's not discuss things over the phone next time."

I acknowledged he was right about that and thanked him for his patience and information. We ended on a nice verbal note and a click of the phone.

My heart was at peace and I felt more certain this might be the right direction to go in with my music. I was amazed that I stayed strong with him on the phone to get the price for the music and to buy myself more time to ponder what exactly I wanted for the money. I want to make sure not to get myself in trouble with another swindler, and this time find the path to working with truly gifted musicians who appreciate me as a person and a woman in the business of music who is singing deeply from her heart. Lauren told me he had a video of his "Vision" tour and would call me to let me know when I could come pick it up and watch it with my friend Laura (or whoever) to see the level of music he was capable of producing. We would then get together and discuss everything more deeply. This sounded good to me. He wasn't pushing me into making any quick commitments to do music business with him, which I was greatly relieved to know. He seemed to be very intelligent, spiritual, and kind toward me; three things I would grow to admire more and more in Lauren as time passed.

The next time I heard from Lauren was around December 29th. He left a message on the house answering machine. I was intrigued to hear him saying he had located the video to watch of his "Vision" tour. He asked if I was up in the area today, and to drop by and pick the video up. I was laughing because Hollywood, where he was located, is an hour drive into the Los Angeles area for me. As a mother with a job and two boys, happening to be in the area of Hollywood would be like a snowball's chance of surviving in Hell. It was not the norm for me, but having a talent and drive to sing, it appeared to be a necessary evolution for me to visit Hollywood.

As it happened, I was available to drive up there to see what he was excited for me to see. It was a bit of proof that he knew something about the business of music in a legitimate way. First, I called Laura to explain what my plan was to have her know where I was going. She was busy and could not go with me. I thought it better to go alone, so this would give me an easy way to pick up the video and leave, making no commitments. I wanted to make any decisions regarding the dollars spent on my career in a slow thoughtful process. For some reason, I felt safe enough to pick up the video and promised Laura if at any time I had hesitation, I would bail out on the whole deal.

I promised to just start with driving up to the area and take a look at where he was located. Laura was nervous for me but understood I was insisting to give it a try to feel out what producer Lauren was about. I ended the conversation on the phone and told her I would call her as soon as I had left the place to come home, and if she did not hear from me by night time, to give the address to the police and come searching for me. She knew I was responsible enough to keep in phone contact no matter what.

Looking back, I'm not sure this was the right thing to do—going alone to anyone's home without better knowledge of the person. In the future, I would recommend meeting at a public place. Sometimes the passion to go forward with a musical career overshadows one's judgment. However, I am proud of setting up a back-up plan with Laura and calling her by a certain time.

I called Lauren after picking up a coffee mocha drink at Seattle's Best. I hoped he would answer and allow me to come by. He answered, and tried to get me to come later in the day. That was not going to work for me because I had to be home for my youngest, who was in third grade. He apologized for his messy house and said, "Okay then, come on by. And oh by the way, my daughter, Candace, is visiting so you'll get to meet her too." This sent a noticeable sense of relief over me. For some reason, the idea of another female, his daughter, being there eased my anxiety about going to Lauren's place by myself.

The hour drive seemed surreal. I was driving to "Hollywood" on Melrose Boulevard. I grew up my whole life in Southern California, but Melrose or Hollywood was never a part of my life. It all felt unbelievable in my mind. Why am I going to where? Then the answer came to mind, "Because you sing as God has intended for you to do so." I was never the "Queen Bee," or center of attention, but instead I was more comfortable doing the legwork behind the scenes, like a worker bee. Today, I was moving forward in the direction of unknown territory, but certain I could not stay hidden in the dark forever with the voice I was blessed with or else it was going to eat me alive.

When I drove by the address Lauren had given me on the phone, it was above a pizza restaurant with a simple big dark green door to the left. I circled the place and parked. I walked down the street and around the corner until I reached the green door. The bizarre nature of the people and the environment was coming across. There was a strange apartment on the corner with people smoking cigarettes, appearing to be in recovery from some substance. There was blaring music coming from across the street in a tattoo store. I walked past an astrology-type store, and then past the pizza place, smelling spicy and good with tiny tables out on the sidewalk. This was just about as different from suburban Orange County as you could get.

I stood at the large green door, knocking to no answer. Puzzled, I called Lauren who told me about the doorbell, which I had overlooked, too distracted by the ambience of the street and the mixture of widely varying individuals passing. Just the differing hair colors and clothing styles had me wide-eyed. I felt for a moment like this was Johnston College again. It was so creative; everyone and everything had an extremely cutting edge feel. This street was on the wave of the future, and it appeared as in a movie. I felt a little stupid banging, and then calling on the cell phone, to get in the magic green door, feeling like Dorothy in the Wizard of Oz, knocking to get in the Emerald city. Suddenly it opened, just enough for Lauren to put his head out, making sure it was me. Neither of us remembered what the other looked like. We only knew each other's voices because of the phone conversations.

It wasn't but a moment before he welcomed me inside. Then we climbed up a very long stairway, me following him as I insisted after he dead bolted the door. His appearance was simple and he appeared friendly. I was on guard, especially hearing the door bolted as I watched to see how he had done this just in case there was a need to escape quickly. The fear factor was building within me but I stabilized myself, listening to him remind me about his daughter being in his home.

At the top of the stairs were doors to the right and to the left. He opened the door to the right and asked me to excuse the mess—a pile of dishes in the sink. Straight in front of the entryway, he showed me into the living room. I was relieved to sit on the antique leopard couch over to one side. I peered curiously around the room, where several beautiful guitars hung on the walls. There was a computer workstation on the left wall with a keyboard; the large pane windows were almost covering the wall ahead with a palm tree or two outside in the distance. Palm trees were a friendly sign because they reminded me of the school bus in high school, which went down a street lined with them. Lauren tried to make me comfortable by asking me if I wanted water, but my nerves were rattled and my heart was pounding.

I was thankful when he soon excused himself to get the video and a small television with a video player. He was excited to see my reaction to the "Vision" video. I felt it would be something worth watching because he spoke sincerely about the fact that the project had been to help others, teenagers. He understood my telling him on the phone the reason to record a CD of my singing was to raise money for charity to help people. The fame or personal riches I don't care about, but to help others in dire straits spoke to my heart deeply as I had experienced being in that position and being the oddball too many times. Helping others and showing kindness has always been an easy thing for me to do. Offering the olive branch of peace to comfort is the greatest treasure we can all give, and is easier than we think.

Lauren told me to have a look around in order to feel comfortable before he had exited the room, so I did shyly walk over to the windows and look down at the American and Italian Flags flying above the Pizza place. This seemed a good sign to me. After all, it was Puck who had knocked on my dorm room door, starting me on the odyssey to become fearless with my singing voice, which lead me to this place in my life now on Melrose Boulevard, above a pizza joint in Hollywood. I giggled a little bit.

Next, I glanced at the numerous beautiful glass trophies lined up. I heard Lauren coming back down the short hall, so I quickly sat back down on the couch on the right side, almost hugging its arm. I rolled my eyes and thought, "Why was I brave enough to come and be here behind two dead-bolted doors with strangers?" I had heard Lauren speaking to someone. I prayed Lauren was a safe person, realizing the danger if he was not. He seemed almost comical lugging the small TV set and trying to get it to work. Finally it started, and I was intrigued and amazed at the quality and the message he was giving out to an audience of junior high children. Lauren again excused himself to leave the room, allowing me to watch the video in peace. It wasn't long before I had the impression this man knew something powerful about the production end of both music and video, or of visual arts. I realized while I was watching the video that Lauren looks like Kurt Russell, or a Kennedy relative (although Brycer now says he looks like, but doesn't act like, Simon Cowell).

After fifteen minutes of a much longer show, the tape shut off unexpectedly because the player malfunctioned. There was an awkward time where I pondered what to do, because I could tell Lauren was not in the next room as there were no sounds coming from anywhere at all. I did not know what to expect sitting in the back part of the house. I tried to think of how to notify him that the player had stopped without getting myself in any traps or unforeseen uncomfortable problems. I decided I would wait on pins and needles, no matter how long until he appeared. I grew more frightened, and debated

whether I been foolish to come into a strange environment with some guy I did not really know? I was

telling myself, "If this man turns evil on me…"

Then Lauren came back into the room, apologizing for the player and trying his best to sooth

what must have been a worried look on my face. He was thinking I felt responsible for the video player.

He had no idea of my history of abuse and the fear that sometimes comes hauntingly over me. He was

such a nice-mannered person, before long I was breathing normally again, but still clutching the side of

the couch.

Lauren began to discuss the video and his producing ability, when in briskly walked

a petite, feminine young lady whose sparkling personality brightened the whole room. She was talking

to her dad, Lauren. He immediately stood up and went and gave her a hug and then kept holding her

next to him. First, he checked on how she was and to see if she wanted breakfast or coffee, while I

looked on more impressed with how he was treating his daughter. I took it as a sign that this man was

trustworthy and this was safe territory for me. A huge wave of calmness came over me as this spunky

little lady talked plainly and simply to her dad.

Lauren introduced me to Candace. She reminded me of my spunky, pretty niece Missy on the

farm, only her appearance was more the Hollywood or "girlie girl" look. Both have smiles that light up

the world. Candace had beautiful blond hair. She was wearing a darling pink top, and had a lovely

Southern Florida accent. I was amazed, because at my house it is all boys and here stood the most fiery

speaking, spiritual, musical, adorably perky, petite young lady holding onto her loving dad. They both

seemed to be sincerely caring people, acting like a typical father would to a beautiful, angel-looking and

spunky-sounding daughter. It brought a smile to my face, which Lauren noticed, so I explained at my house that it was all males. The three of us discussed things for a while until Candace excused her self very politely and left the room.

Now Lauren and I could discuss what my music business needs were with a greater sense of normal conversation and me much less anxious about where I was. We had a cup of coffee, and then I noticed the time, remembering that Laura was going to be praying for my safety and I needed to leave to call her. Besides, I did need to drive the hour back home to put on my mothering hat and be home for my youngest. I explained this to Lauren. He graciously said that was understandable, and then explained he had two children, the other was a son, Christian. Little did I know that name would live in my grateful heart for a lifetime.

We talked about all three of us meeting so he could get a better idea of the direction we wanted to go in with the music, using him as the producer. A producer is in charge of overseeing the engineering, creating the music tracks, the balanced recording mixes between the instruments with my vocals recorded, and mastering the final music to balance perfectly. Before leaving, I set up a tentative next meeting for Sunday, the fourth of January. We agreed on the time and said I would only call if there was a problem making the appointment.

Lauren gave me two copies of the video, one for my partner, Laura, and another for me. He walked me down the long, steep stairway outside his door and back to the sunshine and fresh air. Lauren then closed what now did seem to be a magical green door.

Laura was anxious to know I was safe. I cautiously made a beeline to the safety of my car. Then I called Laura while driving to the freeway along Melrose Boulevard. I explained in detail what had gone on. I told Laura I had thought it was nuts to come alone when Lauren had dead bolted the door, but all and all, everything had worked out very well. I wanted to drive straight to give Laura her video, so I decided to call Joseph to set things up to not be home for the children. I saw Laura and we went out to grab a bite and then returned to her house, but the video player would not work again (technical difficulties). Eventually, I came home in late evening to spend time with the family, trying to share my adventures of the day. I was still thinking over what exactly had transpired and how likely this would be the right moment for me to finally find honest people to create the proper frame for my singing voice and to find its correct home.

Finally, with the children in bed, I tried to go to sleep only to arise shortly after to the realization that, until I watched the entire "Vision" video, there would be no rest for me. I crept quietly out to the living room and slipped in the video. The brief moments of the video that I watched earlier were good enough to intrigue and entice me to watch the rest that night. I sat by myself, grabbing onto a pillow, listening and watching this "Lauren" man who had been in my presence earlier in the day, now on the TV screen performing, talking and singing one powerful song after another. When he sang and spoke of anti-suicide, one huge lonesome tear fell down my cheek as the memories of long ago attempting to take my life floated up from the lost archives of my mind. One thing was definitely true: this man was speaking the truth, "Don't commit suicide. Commit to love."

I wrapped my arms around myself and prayed, thanking God to have come to this point in my life. By the end of the video, I was certain Lauren was in my life and the breeze sailing the ship was picking up. There was a strong feeling, or intuition, that Lauren was sent by God or some higher power. The feelings I was having were a little scary, but mostly they was a long missing peace in my life. I dared not put my hopes too high for fear of all the past disasters, but something changed for me seeing the "Vision Tour" video. Now I was looking back and remembering Lauren's words, saying he didn't know why, but he felt the video was something I had to see. I knew why. It was for the messages he was saying to the junior high school children and the anti-suicide song.

I did reflect back to two months prior. I was coming home from my first Taxi. After being chosen to sing, I finally was ready to let go of something. For almost thirty years, I had kept the razor blade I had used to attempt suicide with even though I didn't exactly know why. I only felt that I was unwilling to part with it. My younger brother had placed the razor blade inside the bathroom cupboard the night I had attempted suicide. Eventually, I had retrieved it and kept this razor blade to remind me never to give up on my life and do such a thing again.

After singing at Taxi, I made the commitment to love myself for the good and the bad, which all goes together. I finally let go, wrapping the blood-stained razor blade in lots of paper towel, burying it deep in the trash and taking the trash out. It was a sense of relief of finally doing what I knew was right. Again I watched the video of Lauren's singing "Somebody Told Me." This removed my doubts that loving myself and committing to love no matter what terrible things happen or I've lived through was a path that I deserved. It made clear that accepting myself for who I am was more important than ever for me to stay alive. That song was a message from God and spurred me on toward perseverance and my dream to sing to help others. With a heart glowing with peace, I watched the end of the video. With praise and thankfulness, I slowly put myself back to bed and gently fell asleep.

The next day, I went to see Laura because I wanted her opinion about the video before calling Lauren back. She watched the video with me smiling, telling me to call Lauren and make an appointment for her and me to speak more in depth about what he had to offer as a producer, and the bottom line: How much money? By the time I arrived back home, it was too late to call—at least that's what I thought because I forgot people working in recording studios are like vampires. They work late into the night often and sleep the early daylight hours away until late afternoon. Musicians work more at night, and recording seems to go along on this schedule. It is rare to know of musicians who get up early in the morning, like six o'clock a.m.

The next day, while in the boys' room sorting clothes from the wash, Lauren called asking if he was interrupting me or if I had a moment to talk. I almost laughed thinking of the typical motherhood job I was performing at the time, which was finishing the wash. I was truthfully more interested in wishing to move the ball along and see what Lauren would have to say. This producer interested me more after having watched a very professional video production with scene changes, multi songs, and a complete package production with the theme of "Vision," standing for anti-violence and clean living for the audience who appeared to be teenagers.

Lauren, the producer, happily discussed the video and the impact it had on me. I conceded he had a work of art musically and visually, with an outstanding meaning. We set up a time on January fourth (about a week away) for Laura and me to have a meeting with him. He was busy working on another project with an artist, so this was the reason for the delay. Now that I was the one in a hurry, the producer Lauren seemed to be hesitating, but he assured me he was definitely interested in trying to work something out to record music for me and respected me for taking my time in the process.

Laura had the same feeling I had when I told her it was going to be awhile before the meeting. Time can go so slow and this was one of those moments, but we took it to mean that God was testing our patience. Besides, it would give us both a chance to refocus and think deeply on what we wanted to do musically for our first professional-quality CD.

Several times I watched the video of "Vision," and pondered what possibilities there were for my musical dreams. I spent time surfing the net to gather any and all information about Lauren, trying hard to make myself educated about this businessman and producer. The picture of him seemed more and more solid, but still my gut was scared of falling back into the pit by making the wrong choice. I promised myself to think clearly every step, no matter how much he seemed the most honest American ever. I was through with believing in mirages when it came to my singing. This time I wanted a chance—

my chance to finally sing without getting into trouble. A chance to raise money for charities using the talent God cast upon me at birth. All I wanted was a chance to sing with my "one voice," and to be at peace finally knowing that I had found the right place for my talent.

I spent part of the week surfing the Internet, investigating what was listed under searches for his name. I read only great things about his accomplishments with this "Vision" tour. I began to understand the reason for his business card having one big eye in the middle. It represented having a "vision," like a dream or positive look toward the future, which I was starting to have moments of flirting with seeing for myself. Still, I was afraid to believe that this person could bring me home to the conclusion of the struggle with my talent.

Laura and I would have a meeting with Lauren. It was to be at eleven o'clock, and we were there right on time that Sunday. Laura was puzzled when I brought her to the green door telling her, "This is it."

Laura giggled, looking at me half smiling, "This is it? Next to a Pizza place? You said it was a green door, and well...this is green." Together, Laura and I felt much safer to navigate the music business.

"Trust me, we will be okay," I shook my head side to side, rolling my eyes, puzzled that I was standing for the second time in front of this huge solid green door with windows up above to the right, which I remembered looking out of when previously visiting this home studio.

Suddenly, the door burst open to show Lauren who greeted us both, acting very politely. He asked us in a friendly way to come in, and I lead the way up the stairs. It was two chicks with some guy on an odyssey to find where the music is happening. I was more at ease than Laura. I still had the good memory of being there with Candace, Lauren's sweet daughter, and safely leaving for home. Laura was trusting in me to know how to handle the situation.

Lauren welcomed us into the studio in his living room and offered us coffee and water.

Apologizing, he admitted being a bachelor without much else in his refrigerator. We both said, "Thank you," but we just wanted to get down to discussing music and the professional business of recording. Lauren wanted to know what we were looking for. I did most of the talking as Laura sat quietly, adding only an occasional word to back me up. We guardedly discussed what our vision was at the time concerning music. Minutes passed into hours. Time was sailing by as the picture was painted more clearly of our dream to record highly top-notch music.

After about an hour, I felt comfortable enough to allow Lauren to hear some prior records to get the idea of my vocal ability and Laura's as well. He heard the music, and there was a light of recognition across his face when hearing the width of my range. He looked at me saying, "That's you? Or that's what you would like to sing like?"

I glanced sheepishly at Laura momentarily, and then looking back at Lauren said, "No that's me singing. I have been singing like that ever since I can remember and now I can't take it any more. I just want to sing and raise money for charity if that's possible and God's will."

Laura piped up, smiling, "That's her. She's a singer."

I spoke back to Lauren stating, "She does, too. Beautifully, in a nice warm Latin accent way. So good you just want to wrap yourself around her vocals."

Both Laura and I knew we were quoting words spoken a long time ago by others our paths had crossed. I was quoting the big producer who had heard us. Lauren then heard the Christmas song Laura and I recorded, as we explained the extremely quick timing of learning the song to be recorded almost too fast. This time he acknowledged getting the capacity of Laura's vocals to only question if this was the musical style we wanted to be working in. Laura and I shook our heads telling him no, we want modern cutting edge music, R & B. I told him we want to fly vocally on the crest along the wave of music being played on the current radio today.

We declined to sing much of anything in person beforehand, and had decided before the meeting I would watch Laura's face and set the pace as to how much information we would discuss with him. Caution did not begin to say what the atmosphere was in the room. Lauren was quick, lively, and very friendly; then I would speak, watching his reaction to try and weed out anything that would send up a red flag to stop talking with him. Having been burned badly before with a so-called "producer" or recording studio owner (Mr. Egg Dolly), I wanted nothing to do with anyone like him. Laura left it up to me as to how long the meeting would go. At each turn, Lauren endured my intense focus and questioning, always bringing it back to the money and what the promises would be. He mentioned signing a contract before working with someone, and I questioned this in detail, although I thought the idea was a good one. After a couple hours, I told the story about the Mr. Dolly crime incident and Lauren genuinely showed concern even though I softened the abuse issue, not giving the details at that time of what inspired me to create the lyrics to the song.

At one point early on, as Lauren was sitting on the windowsill, he made a plain statement, "No matter how great you sing, and you sing great, don't get me wrong—if at your mature age you don't have a gimmick or something that sets you apart, the likelihood of success is much less."

Laura looked at me sadly, feeling shot down. Soon I spoke up saying, "I have my Master's Degree in Humanistic and Transpersonal Psychology. I study why people are inhibited to sing or be creative in any way. That is what I specialize in, and it's not a gimmick. It's my life."

Lauren turned his profiled face toward me quicker than he ever has or ever will. It almost shocked me how fast, in fact. "What did you just say? Tell me some more about that, please."

It was scary how these simple true words always caught people's attention, and I never was so glad to have attended Johnston College mostly because I was self-assured to speak with Lauren because of speaking with professors of great status on a one-on-one basis. I embraced Johnston's philosophy of using everyone's first name and standing firm in the belief that we are all of equal value in our own ways.

Lauren now had the puzzled look, asking me to repeat myself as he stood up and walked closer to Laura and me sitting on the couch.

Laura quickly said, "She has her Master's in psychology! It was like she had found the get out of jail card.

The mighty producer was listening intensely as I slowly confirmed the truth of my hidden expertise about music and healing. I explained my college background and intense inhibition to sing. Lauren was intrigued by my words, or so it seemed by his follow-up questions. We sorted out what I was truly about. Not just a singer or a girl with a dream to be famous, but a woman compelled to investigate the journey of the psychology of the singer, music, and creativity. On and on I accepted the labels, feeling deep inside that I was the simple girl addicted to singing, like my childhood nickname bestowed on me: "Snow White."

It was too long before Lauren said, "Well, I'll tell you what you need to do: write an autobiographical book about music and healing and every chapter title can be the name of a song on a CD."

His one sentence changed my life. It was like the piece to the puzzle missing for decades. I had, at graduation for my Master's, wanted to write a book about music and healing, but this idea of an autobiography tied into a CD of songs was like the jackpot coming in. It was like Lauren was sending me a message from God, which unstuck my musical spirit in a huge way. It was such a Johnston College type idea with an amazing slant on the music. I knew he had just said something to change my life, but little did I know how big a mountain this would be until months later. This felt like watching a man stepping on the moon, only I was the man and was stepping into my life's work. Now I was the one asking, "What did you just say?"

Laura said, "No, we want to record music."

What Lauren had said hit a nerve in me that was deep within my gut. I turned to Laura after hearing Lauren's thoughts repeated for a second time and remarked, "Yeah." Then she said, "Yeah? Okay write a book. She already has one."

I corrected her, telling Lauren I had written a major paper (equivalent to a thesis) at my college, along with a twenty-song, one-woman show I performed. The paper was on music and healing and was never put into a book, but it was the definite start of a music and healing book.

Lauren spoke about the idea of him working on the music to accompany the book and more of how my story of living with this talent within me and the series of struggles I have gone through to be documented in my writings. He gave his input as to how this book could be a self-help type thing, where others see they are not alone and should follow their creative dreams. A few times, he suggested I get a ghostwriter or pay an English student to write my story. Calmly I told him, "No, I will write the book, but will have to find a final editor."

Lauren asked me to tell him more of what I had studied in school, so I went into a more broken-down explanation of my journey starting to investigate my inhibitions to sing.

Finally, I excused myself to use the bathroom. I took a moment there to look in the mirror, realizing the missing link for almost thirty years had fallen into my lap. I was going to write a book about music and healing from an autobiographical slant and record songs to fit each chapter. This man Lauren was brilliant, and my life had a renewed sense of meaning. I prayed for calmness, thanksgiving, and my future of helping others. When I returned to the living room, Laura and Lauren were now talking. This time, I sat down on the chair across from Lauren instead of the couch because the setting sun coming in the window had been bothering my eyes on the side of the couch where I had been up until then.

Lauren was sitting down opposite of me with Laura on the antique couch closer to me. Lauren started saying he saw four ways this music and image could be taken. First, you could have the image with music of the whole natural "jean skirt, turquoise jewelry thing" going on, with boots perhaps too. "Kind of like a hippie rock image," he said, looking my way.

I declined this quickly, stating clearly, "Although it's not something I would never wear." Laura agreed.

Next, he said, "Well you could do the whole "evening gown, formal image" look, with hair fixed up nicely."

I turned this down even quicker, explaining, "It's not that I wouldn't ever wear a formal gown, but it would almost take an act of God for me to wear a dress. I'm just not a 'girlie girl' type. I would never think of frilly girlie clothes as my favorite career outfit. I can feel comfortable wearing something feminine and lady-like, but it has to have class and I can't wear it all the time. I'm part tomboy or realistic woman in my attire."

Laura spoke up, giggling, "I'm the glamour girl."

Lauren brought up the idea of us being a Gospel group and how big this type of music was becoming. He was going on about these three images, especially the natural turquoise thing. Laura asked him what he saw her wearing, curious with her modeling history.

I knew image as a performer was important. I was more interested in the singing then the fashion show part of being a performer. Quickly, I interrupted and excused myself, quizzing him, "What's the fourth one?" He looked at me, surprised. None of his other three image ideas had caught my attention, but the idea of fourth had. I pressed him again for the answer.

"The fourth one," he said, "Would be more of a risk." He was speaking slowly, looking at Laura and then me. I was pressing again for the answer to "what's behind door number four?" Lauren said, "That would be the wild card! Most people never take that, because they want more of a sure thing, like one of the other three I mentioned." Lauren spoke to me sitting in a chair, negotiating with him several feet away, looking eye to eye with me.

As soon as I heard him stop talking, and with the likes of a straight-faced poker player, I said, "I'll take the wild card."

He tried to correct my thinking, warning me, "It's not as much wilder as taking a chance versus a more sure thing. With the voice you have, using one of the other three, it would be hard not to sell some significant amount of records."

I looked at him and said, "Playing it safe is usually what would interest me, but maybe that's why I'm here at the age I am, still wanting to do something with the talent God blessed me with. I'll take the wild card and do a little bit of whatever it is seems to be the right style and songs. I'm a genre buster. I don't want to be pigeon-holed into any one arena with my voice, at least not yet. Can you help me? Will you still be willing to record me?"

Lauren grew a smile across his face. I knew he was respecting me for my choice, which he remarked, admiring my guts to take a chance.

I told him, "At my age, it's about time I did." I would wear what I wanted when it seemed appropriate, being much more interested in the singing and music than wearing clothes to impress anyone. What is inside a person counts to me, not the dressings on the window, although it is fun to dress up or wear an image for fun. I just believe it's important not to take yourself too seriously for all the wrong, vain reasons.

Eventually, Lauren told me that, based upon my intense scrutiny of him today, he thought I would be capable of writing a book and recording a CD, but it would be a huge undertaking. He chuckled and I knew he was complimenting me, even though I felt shy to have taken up three hours of his time without any firm deal. At this point, Lauren asked if I knew why I would be so shy or inhibited to sing with such a great voice. For moral support I glanced at Laura. I decided to let this man, Lauren, closer into my world and told him how being sexually abused at five years old had put a deep-seated fear in me that was triggered sometimes by my singing. I explained how for decades I had subconsciously felt uncomfortable about being singled out for abuse again because of my singing. Talking to Lauren, I was trying desperately not to shed a tear because I was afraid I might not be able to stop.

Finally, at sunset, we discussed music deeper as I now sat again on the couch beside Laura. Lauren quickly said, "Hold on a minute." He swung his computer chair over to his electric keyboard and started playing chords to a beautiful melody. Then he turned to explain that the conversation had made him think of a song he had written when first coming out to Hollywood. He was offering to play it, and we liked the idea of hearing his talent live. I had been more open to discussing the nature of the abuse after Lauren had asked a second time for the details of the song stolen from me. Laura and I looked at each other, both feeling the song he would play would have meaning relative to my childhood abuse.

Slowly Lauren began, fingers dancing on the keyboard. A lovely melody poured out. Singing with a beautiful voice, "You hold to on possessions. You hold on to your past. You hold on to the painful things that hold your future back. You hold on to the memories afraid to let them go, but until you do, you're never gonna know."

The haunting words cut deep into my aching, abused, frustrated, and lonely soul. Then the chorus came, uplifting my heart toward the light of peace,

"If you want to fall in love you must let go. And if you want to fall in love you must let go. This life you live, the love you give will soon return to show. If you want to fall in love you must let go..."

Instantly, one lone tear fell very slowly down my cheek, Laura, seeing this gave me a gentle calming touch as a friend supporting me. The rest of the song was my story. I thought, "How could this stranger know so much about me or shed light upon my weary spirit without knowing me? It must be God and this song, "Let Go," by Lauren Stalnecker. To me, it was the hand of God encouraging me to "Let Go," and trust this was the right direction to go. To "Let Go" and sing with more might than ever, and fall in love with my passion to sing again. The key to awesome heavenly singing, I realized, was to "Let Go," and to follow the beauty of your dreams and away from the trauma or abuse. "Let Go" and have faith in yourself with God's love to heal.

Afterwards, Lauren, surprised by my reaction of being so deeply touched, asked if I was okay and offered me water. I accepted, more out of shock from what a beautiful song this man had just sung in a lovely multi-talented way than of the thirst in my mouth. I felt a quenching within my spirit by the music he had played. When he returned with the water, I asked Lauren if I paid him to record me, could hat be one of the songs? He was a little caught off guard by my question, telling me he had not

performed it for me to try to get me to record it. He had just been moved by my words of expressing my

abuse and the journey of my life to play the song. I insisted that it would have to be one of the songs,

because it's me. Laura agreed that the lyrics portrayed my life. The lyrics to the song reflected my

thinking about how I treated others with great caring and love, especially when they are in times of

need.

The song "Let Go" will forever remind me to let go of all the pain from my childhood, including

the sexual abuse, being teased, and being told not to sing. Letting go of pain is a process we all work on

through out our lives, and with God's love and faith, it is possible, one moment at a time. Singing "Let

Go" helps me to let go of the horrible recurring feelings from being abused, too. I felt that night that no

matter the cost, I must record this song.

Shortly after performing, Lauren said a prayer for us all and we parted company. We left to walk

to my car. Both Laura and I were analyzing the time spent with Lauren, the producer. My mind kept

drifting to the song, "Let Go." I drove slowly down Melrose Boulevard to the freeway, dropped Laura off

an hour later, and then drove home for another half an hour. Still, the song and performance by Lauren

circled my spirit. We had agreed with him to call and talk about the details of money soon if we were

going to use him.

I waited a few days just to give time for us to have some space and breathing room without

making any rushed decisions that we might later have regretted. This time had to be different than the

path I had been on before, as my energy could not take any more dead ends or pain.

Finally, holding my breath, I dialed Lauren's phone number. He answered, which caught me off

guard. He sounded anxious to have me agree to a CD. Instead, I insisted we meet to go over the contract

papers that Lauren said he always signed with his clients. I thought the idea of signing an agreement ahead of recording was a great one, but I wanted time to look over any contract. I pondered what Lauren's expectations would be in writing. I had to have time for Rue to look over everything first. Lauren was pressured to get back to working in the studio, so he gave in to me pretty easily and we set up a time. It was the middle of January—the eleventh—2004.

The day came quickly when again I was driving down Melrose Boulevard with Laura to a recording studio in a loft above a pizza joint. This time when I called, Lauren called down from above to acknowledge us, and arrived quickly to let us in the magic green door. Up the long stairs we climbed, entering his living room studio area. After Lauren politely offered us coffee or water, we all three sat down to talk about the music business.

We had not talked for too long when Lauren asked us if we would mind finishing our conversation in his kitchen over coffee. He explained there was someone who needed to use his recording equipment. We took no offense to moving, and I accepted his offer this time of coffee. He brought us the several papers of the contract he used for signing with other artists and left us for a minute, so Laura and I talked quietly. I scanned the papers, impressed by the format and what was being said. Laura and I were both nervous and trying hard not to show this. Soon Lauren came back in, sincerely apologizing. He was hard to figure out. Was he really this nice, kind, and professional of a person, or was he just a spider looking for the next fly?

Painstakingly, line-by-line, Lauren read the contract, explaining and answering my questions. At times, Laura would look questioningly toward me, and I filled in her thoughts by giving examples of why this was a good contract. Lauren almost didn't know what to make of my doing this, I felt. My concern was about making sure there were no pitfalls, empty or missing items, or snakes within the lines of the contract. I was pleasantly amazed to see that Lauren was being honest, and I was relieved inside, yet cool on the outside.

There was still the question of how to come up with the money before going forward. The cost to record three songs would be a few thousand. This was to include the instrumentation, done to our approval, and as many takes of the vocals as we thought were needed. It was to be a flat fee instead of charging per hour for studio time. By the end, poor Lauren was dead tired of trying to paint himself in a good and trustful light. He honestly rested his thoughts, having nothing more to say. I felt sorry for putting him through the negotiating process, but we both acknowledged that if this went ahead, it would be great music and a great business transaction, too.

We parted amicably, agreeing he would hear from us soon either way to let him know our plans. Leaving, I said a prayer of thanks that my father had taught me how to negotiate. I had been a steady rock on the outside, even if inside I felt differently. Laura was amazed I knew so much about contracts, which was only because of the past pain with the rotten Egg Dolly.

Laura and I played it cool, walking downstairs and around the corner and outside, but as soon as we were on the next street, we chattered about our options. I was pondering the contract papers, still clutched in my hands like gold. This man had shown me an honest and fair recording contact. He had blown me away. I had half expected him to show me a junk contract and the options of working with him would be over; but no, he was still very much in the race as a producer. Wow!

Driving home, Laura and I discussed everything again. Did we like his idea? Why the wild card? Where would we get the money? Laura was still not working. I was working at the title company. Laura had time, being younger than me. I felt that the time was now, and didn't want to wait any longer. I only wanted honest, kind, caring people who would give me a chance to have a say and be able to bring me the top quality music I knew was possible to be created.

The following night, Laura and I went to the Songwriter's Guild in LA again to hear a speaker. The main speaker had written a very popular book on the music business and was teaching classes at a prestigious college. We heard the ideas he presented and looked into joining the Songwriter's Guild of America, which has branches all over the USA. It seemed like a wealth of great information and support. We left impressed with the organization and having the desire to meet again with this music book writer.

We did eventually have a quick dinner with him, where he insisted we had to buy his meal. The information he gave us on our ideas were negative and he seemed to be very narrow-minded, which was unsettling, because at one time he was the innovator that wrote a cutting edge book, opening up about his experiences about the music business. He now seemed locked into his views and thoughts, which were the only way. This didn't sit well for me. It was the beginning of my realizing that to be original or fresh means sometimes going against those who should support you, because they forged their way down a new path and now can't see the tree from the forest. I felt proud of myself for having the courage to define myself and not listen to this successful, yet cocky and negative person. I have since found that the most successful people are like my father, and are unafraid to empower another person to be different in the direction of their passions. The best thing we can do is take the time to not just hear someone, but to listen to their ideas.

Laura and I left our discussion over Lauren's proposed business papers to see what Rue would say about the contract. Two days later, I took it to her. Rue had signed numerous contracts in her time as a star. She was a brilliant person who read everything and said, "What you have here is a great contract, not the junk Mr. Dolly had tried to get you to sign. I think you have good instincts now, and if you believe his music quality is tops, go for it!"

Rue and I discussed the options and the money that would have to be paid. It became clearer that I had a way to come up with the money and a willingness to go into partial debt to start up a business. Laura hesitated more to take a chance, and her finances were not the same as mine. I didn't want to think of doing just my own thing recording-wise, because Laura and I had become close friends.

I ended up also calling Matt, who had recorded both Laura and I, to ask his professional opinion of the money being charged to do three songs. He questioned what I thought of the quality of the work this producer was able to do. He assured me that my opinion of the producer's work was a solid one with my impressive talent for singing. He said it was not the highest price and not the cheapest, but that is sounded like a fair price. He stated that any great recording by a producer would cost at least a couple thousand per song, maybe a little less. If it's too cheap a price, the quality will show in the final recordings.

I understood that from my past experiences where the instrumentation was not matching the quality of my vocal talent. The songs were always great, but there was something not as perfect instrumentation-wise, and this affected the entire presentation of the song. This time, even if the money was a lot more, I felt it was important to have my voice finally recorded professionally.

Laura met me after Rue's at Red Lobster restaurant for tea. We talked a long time, and she insisted I not take any chances with trying to pay for a whole CD with her included. I finally agreed it was the more sensible thing to just have a go with Lauren's producing ability by recording me singing three songs. One would have to be "Let Go" for me to go forward and trust Lauren's word in saying I could record this song. Driving home, I felt lonely but happy to see where my future with music would be and I prayed. No more pain, God.

The next day, I pondered and prayed again. I picked up Lauren's card and placed it back on my keyboard. Finally, I called to tell him of the decision. At first, I explained that my partner was not able to come up with the money. Hearing his disappointment, my words were, "If I record a three song deal with you, can I for sure have "Let Go" be the first one?"

It was a surprised voice that spoke back to me from Lauren saying, "Yes, if you feel that strong about singing it." He urged me to come soon to bring him a down payment on the recording of the song. I would pay a third before he would give me a music track, then a third more when recording the vocals, and a third when the final mix was finished and ready for me to pick up. I offered to drive up that day, but he said in a couple of days was fine. We both sounded relieved by the end of the conversation.

I went up to the studio on January 22, a late Friday afternoon. I met with Lauren and brought him a basket of iced decorated cookies in the shape of musical instruments with the name of his two children and himself. Lauren had mentioned to Laura and I that he wanted to get to know, on a deep level, anyone he is writing or producing music for—strictly on a non-intimate level, just to have a greater feeling of the artist. I was impressed by his thoroughness and his professional attitude.

So I brought a gift to show what it is I love to do most. I enjoy doing random acts of kindness or caring for others often with a unique idea. I love lending a hand where I see the need without being asked. Thoughtfulness, understanding, kindness, unconditional love, and caring are very important to me; it always has been and always will be. Sometimes I spend money to do this. Other times, I simply open a door for an elderly person or say "Hello!" or "Great job!" to a person in my journey through life. For me, the cookie basket was a way to show who I was to Lauren. It is hard for me to be greedy or unthankful. I just don't get why people can be like that. Some might label me stupid, silly, or naïve, but I would call them blind—too blind to see the rewards of kindness.

We briefly discussed ideas for another two songs, one having to do with some type of sing-along song I wanted to record. He attempted to key the song "Let Go" to give him an idea of where the starting note for the song would be best for my vocals. I told him of my desire to co-create a song with lyrics expressing the reasons or ways to sing. Lauren was agreeable, telling me to write my ideas down or a future song. He encouraged me to first write an outline for the book, too. Soon our business meeting was over, and I was back on Melrose Boulevard, making a beeline to my car and heading home.

On Sunday, January 24, arriving back at Melrose Boulevard and the loft studio, I signed a five-page contact with Lauren. We both agreed upon having a nice, young, bright gentleman named Greg witness the contract signing. That was when my dream ship of life set sail on the big open waters of the recording business, full speed ahead and all hands on deck. My nerves were frayed, but I was back in the race. Again, I brought a humble gift of some token food to offer thanks for being a guest. Lauren was very appreciative, and I the same when he handed me the first music instrumentation track for my first professional song, "Let Go," by Lauren Stalnecker. I was the better for what he gave to me and I was humbled to know he had enjoyed receiving a fun musical cookie gift basket.

There was just one very unnerving moment soon after signing for a three-song demo. A few other people had shown up to the loft, and when I walked back into the living or studio room, I was introduced to a young Asian girl. She was very petite and cute with dark hair. Lauren excused himself from the room. Quickly, this young woman was close and in my face, quizzing me about my doing one song with Lauren. I corrected her and said it was to be three songs. She at point blank, stared at me and said, "He will only be doing one song with you, you'll see."

I was in shocked, trying hard to act calm, but alarm bells were going off inside. The introductions had been so quick with this girl that I didn't recall if she was an artist or not. Why was she so negative and certain that he was going to record only one song with me? The serious question was, am I going to be taken financially and had I just signed papers that would end up meaning nothing? I was very confused. Lauren had stressed for me to trust him. He asked me to listen only to him as my producer and not any negative junk other people might say. I just hadn't expected it to come so soon or to be from someone standing in his studio.

Lauren came back and I left, still struggling to be happy with the decision to have signed the papers and given him quite a bit of money. I prayed and held close to my faith in God. Walking down the stairs to the green door was a slow process this time. I was having déjà vu. I was wondering if I had been there before. I wanted to sit on the steps and cry, but my anxious body kept moving.

On January 25, I made my first payment to Lauren of one thousand, five hundred dollars. I held my breath and prayed. I felt at the age of forty-seven, after having endured and survived a life time of challenges, it was time to invest in myself with the God-given talent bestowed upon me at birth. Without the support of my family or parents, I was jumping off the cliff of "playing it safe" to trust in God's love and guidance more than ever before.

I went up to Lauren's loft studio on January 29, 2004. The golden musical ship had started to go forward again. This day I was to meet Lauren's son, who was to be engineering and working on my project too. I was hoping his son had the same strong, self-assured, intelligent attitude with a deep heart like his sister, Candace.

On February 3, I received an email from Lauren. That same day, I had driven home from Rue's, and my car had broken down, needing to be towed. The music track, now in the right key for the first song, "Let Go," was ready for pick up. It wasn't long before I had visited with Lauren to pick up the music track for "Let Go," paying him the third of the money to start a three-song CD. I took it to Rue, who noticed immediately the connection between the words and my life. This song would be great for me to let go and hit some of my top notes. I could express my love of singing through this meaningful and lovely song.

He asked me to come up in the evening, saying his son and partner would be able to come and I could meet him. I showed up first, but shortly thereafter walked in a tall, good-looking young man who Lauren introduced to me as his other child, Christian.

Christian was very polite and energetic, with a lovely smooth Florida country accent, telling his dad of his day's adventure, which instantly showed me how close they were. I felt a little overwhelmed with the extroverted two of them and timid me, so I gave myself time and prayed to feel relaxed soon. First, I insisted they both hear my vocal of the song stolen by Mr. Dolly. I wanted them to understand what I was truly capable of, so if we all agreed to work together with the money that was paid, the quality of my singing would be at this top level.

Christian was more interested to just get going making music, but his father explained that it is important for us to hear from our client before she agrees to work with us. Lauren tried to play the song on his studio mixing computer, but the track refused to play, which he remarked was odd and that he never had a track that was unwilling to play.

Again, I insisted he had to hear just the one stolen song, saying, "When you hear the song, it will be evident why. It's the range, the vocal tone and the quality of the lyrics."

Christian said he was almost spooked when he saw that there was a problem with the computer. He was looking straight at me and I felt part of his unsettled feelings were because of seeing my anguish-engulfed face. He mentioned something like, "Dad, maybe we need to pass on working with this client."

Since Lauren had previously heard the details about this stolen song, he understood what the sad look on my face was about. Quickly he declined Christian's suggestion.

Christian asked me, "Are you spiritual?"

"What?" I asked him, wanting this friendly polite young man to say those beautiful words so often lacking in people's minds, especially sometimes with younger individuals.

Again puzzled, Christian asked, "Are you spiritual? You know, do you believe in God or Christ?"

This time I said, "Am I spiritual? You bet! Or else I wouldn't be sitting here right now. I would be dead." The stolen song was playing now in the background. The minute the song started,

I could see Lauren's ears were intensely listening. I said not one word, but saw the calm, happy expressions on those two as the song grew to its climax with the double high note ending, showing my full range.

When Lauren walked across the small room toward Christian, I had a strong gut feeling and

a growing sensation of energy within the room. This energy sensation seemed vaguely visible in a circular pattern that soon encompassed the three of us. I couldn't help but take notice of this round energy field that had no other explanation; it was like lighting in the room. I felt it had to be the love of God there and sensed we three were being protected from the evil of the past. Christian questioned his Dad, Lauren, "Do you feel that strong presence with us here?" Lauren looked at Christian and acknowledged calmly saying, " yes." We three spent a silent moment making eye contact and looking around the perimeters of the circle and the edges of the entire room. They never said anything more to what Christian had referenced and I never did either. I continued to think, who are these two guys sharing this intense circular beam of energy with me as it is clearly still cradling us three? Then Christian said, "What do you think that means?" Lauren answered, "That we need to help her in any way we can." Those words from Lauren rang in my being and it was as if he read my mind that this energy, or field of God's love, present in that room was a clear sign God was protecting me and these two men were sent from something more Almighty than anything there is, or ever will be, or has ever been.

By the end, Christian and Lauren had asked me a few times, "That's you? That was you singing?"

The tears in my eyes said it all, and I kept shaking my head up and down yes. The pieces to the puzzle of why it had been so important for them to hear became very clear.

I explained to Lauren why I never allowed him to hear the song before, and he understood my pain and explained the details to Christian. I felt from their reaction that they would never do such a cruel thing to me. Then sweet Christian said, "Well, I can and want to help you if you'll let me. Listen to something I worked on making up earlier." He played a loop of music that had me up, dancing, and thrilled just listening to it.

I danced shyly to the music with my face pointed to a speaker and ears listening closely. He just wanted to give me an idea of his groove and the type of sound he's capable of producing. It was loop music, which is computerized, preprogrammed music that is repeated and then built into a melodic or rhythmic song.

Years prior, when I had a routine hearing check, I was told my left ear hears more high range sounds and my right ear hears more low range sounds. It seems that when I want to listen to something closely, I tilt my left ear close, and then the right one to listen well. It was something I had noticed myself doing, but after this hearing test, it made sense as to why. One of the most important keys to great singing is a great ear for listening. This is not to say that if you are deaf, singing is not possible. Deaf people use other senses to navigate this world. Everyone should sing sounds of some sort, but fine-tuning your singing means listening intuitively and using your ears to hear in a strong and focused way. When the song is ready to record, it is about singing and listening all in one moment.

Standing to my right, Christian leaned toward me, commenting positively about the music and the groove. Lauren stood to his right, with all three of us in a line around the computer playing the music loop track. They both seemed a little pensive for my reaction. It wasn't long before

Christian was improvising sounds, singing along and demonstrating for me one of his styles of music.

Soon, I questioned, "Can I have this as one of my songs to record?"

There was a feel about the beat and the melody that hitting upon my spirit in a bright way. At first, Christian pressed that he would create even better music for me. Then he understood my enthusiasm for the exact melodic music and agreed to compose a full song for me to record as one of the three songs. I started improvising scat, playing vocally to the melody jumping the octaves up then sliding down as I danced facing the speaker. The music was comforting to my soul. Eventually, Lauren excused himself from the room because his cell phone rang. Awhile later, Christian turned off the music to ask me more questions about what kind of music I wanted to have produced. He quizzed me as what genres or styles of music were my favorites.

We were interrupted by his cell phone, which I insisted he answer. I walked toward the tall, long windowpanes on one wall, and stared out far off where two lonely palm trees stood within the cement city of Hollywood. I contemplated and prayed while looking down on Melrose Boulevard out the windows on the front of the loft building. My thoughts were about my future musical recordings, and the potential of this was dancing happily about in my head.

Christian got off the phone quickly and stood next to me in the small room. As Christian approached the window, he was talking music composition in a technically hip way. When I first met Christian, I noticed part of a tattoo peeking out of the right arm of his short sleeve shirt. I asked, "You have a tattoo?" Christian, serious, but in a joking manner, confessed to having several tattoos and a piercing in his ear as well, ending by saying he can do music that rocks! Pointing to the image barely visible on his upper right arm, I timidly asked, "What is that tattoo a picture of, on your arm?"

"The cross of my savior, Jesus, Ma'am!" Christian humbly replied.

"Can I see your cross?" I spoke, wondering if he was teasing me or telling the truth.

I gazed, amazed at this healthy, handsome young man.

"You want to see this one?" he continued, grabbing his shoulder with his opposite hand.

"Yes, if you don't mind. I've never seen what a cross of Jesus tattoo looks like," I curiously remarked.

Christian lifted his right sleeve. "Yes Ma'am. See, it is the cross, but there is no Jesus because he needs to be within everyone and me, since he is risen. You know what I mean by that?" Christian was very impressive to me, speaking these spiritual words and sounding pleasant with his slight Southern accent too.

"Yes, risen indeed."

I smiled at Christian and started to feel safer by the second. I began to humbly hold onto the idea that finally God had delivered me to the place where at last my singing voice would be respected along with me as a human being, too. I gazed in wonderment at the beautiful image of an ornate cross tattoo on this spiritual young man. It covered a large area of his upper arm, about five inches.

I suddenly remembered the first tattoo I ever saw—my Uncle Dale's ship's anchor. It had been in the same place, right upper arm. He was tattooed sometime while serving in the Navy during World War II. To me, this was a clear sign from God to trust going in this direction with my musical dreams with Christian and Lauren. Christian was the messenger for me that this was a trusting place, filled with unconditional love. Christian's intricate cross became my favorite tattoo, healing some of the painful loss of my uncle who had long passed away.

Christian's was the most inspirational tattoo I had ever seen. I expressed to Christian that the tattoo seemed respectful and spiritual to me and I believed Jesus would say the same. I was deeply impressed by Christian's lovely explanation of what it meant to him by wearing this particular tattoo.

Smiling with relief, I remarked how impressed I was to see a tattooed cross instead of the pirate's skull or poison.

Lauren walked back into the studio/living room apologizing, but then stopped with eyes wide open in disbelief. He appeared to be shocked. Lauren saw Christian from the back as he held up his right sleeve. I gazed at Christian's tattoo, facing Lauren's direction to see his fully exposed tattooed upper arm. Lauren snapped out quickly, "Christian, what are you doing? Showing her your tattoo? What are you thinking?! This is our client!" Lauren anxiously spoke in a fatherly, concerned manner to Christian.

I instantly defended Christian and admitted and accepted any wrongdoing was my fault. "I asked to see it. It's okay he's not doing anything wrong. It's just that I have never seen a cross tattoo and I asked him to let me see." I felt like a little schoolgirl in trouble with the teacher for sharpening my pencil too much. I was confused at what the big deal was.

Then I understood; Lauren was still trying to make a deal for me to do music with Christian and him. I reassured him the deal for doing music was on for sure, and having seen this cross was a clear good sign to me. I felt embarrassed to have caused the whole ruckus and tried desperately to take the blame. Finally, I said, "After all, I'm the client and it's just a tattoo on his arm."

Lauren attempted to calm his worry over his son's actions or what he thought was improper at the time. Now he realized his son was not offensive to me. Lauren didn't know that seeing this tattoo image of the cross only bolstered my confidence in Lauren as my producer and in his son's musical skills too. Maybe this time God was leading me to higher ground and caring, sincere, spiritual, and musically talented blessed people who truly appreciated where all great creative skills come from. Just the chances that this could be really true made me feel weak in the knees.

Soon after, several young friends of Christian started showing up at the studio. This time, Lauren offered to walk me downstairs to check the safety of the outside for me. We stood on the Melrose Boulevard Sidewalk, right outside the dark green magic door, talking for a short time. Lauren again apologized for the tattoo ordeal. I smiled, impressed by Lauren's formal attitude upon me seeing his son's branded upper arm. Again, I reinforced that it was my insistence to see the tattoo, not Christian's. I softly pleaded, "I'm the client, so please forget about it." More relaxed, we both agreed to drop the whole thing.

Lauren went on to speak about the high quality of music I would be recording. It felt like he was again attempting to talk me into using him as a producer when he already had the job. Then he told me, "The person who will be really doing the music for you is that young man up there: Christian, my son. He's very gifted at building today-sounding music tracks and engineering recordings." Lauren pointed to the same long white windows I had previously stared out of earlier.

I gazed up at amazement of this entire event, marking a turn in my life. Strongly, I felt Lauren was conscientious and seemed to be what was needed for my music project. I reflected on what my successful businessman father would be saying if he was in my shoes now. This was a great first business meeting with Christian and Lauren Stalnecker.

Soon, Christian called out the window down to his father. I could tell that they both kept tabs on where or what the other was up to, which impressed me too. It was evident to me they were close as a father and a son. Lauren looked up at Christian and said, "I'll be there soon. Go ahead and start making music without me." Then, Christian's head disappeared back inside the tall, long, open window, and Lauren looked me in the face. "That's really who will be producing you!" Lauren confessed, "That kid you just saw—my son—is great at doing music with the cool, hip, grooving sound going on. He's going to be the one who works with you, okay?"

I felt nervous, as if this was the first move to cheat me, because my guard was way up for anything like that. "I signed papers for you to produce me, not your son. I want you to do the job of producing."

My father's negotiating skills leaped from my mouth. Calm, but frightened inside, I stood up for what was agreed to in writing. Lauren at first tap-danced around the technicality of whom or what "producer" meant. I asked for co-producing rights as I had been doing now. We agreed I would be executive producer over the whole project. Lauren would be my music producer. Christian would be a strong force in building the music tracks and engineering me while recording my vocals. I agreed, but only as long as Lauren promised to always be present when I recorded. My biggest worry was that my father would not respect me for working with a very young person who was also a little wild. I believed my father would respect me more for putting my trust and faith in Lauren, since he was a mature-aged man. I thought it would help me to be considered "more legitimate" by my father and others if I worked with Lauren on a business level to record music. Seeing my concern and talking my thoughts over, Lauren gave me his promise to always be the producer and oversee and be in the room whenever I recorded, even if Christian would be doing the production and recording of most everything. I was feeling satisfied with this arrangement.

My hesitation to have just Christian working with me was his young age of twenty-four and the youthful sense of his personality. I felt that this might swallow me up, and again my thoughts about the direction of a song would be ignored as they had often been in the past with other engineers. Christian had a quality I knew would be an asset to building music tracks. I had some concerns that if I wasn't directed in a focused way, I might not be able to record my vocals to their highest level. I believe it's important creative individuals stay focused.

There were brief moments with Christian when I hadn't quite known if he was serious or joking. At the age I was and the place in time, there was no patience left in me to work with difficult musicians who would not allow me to have a part in the creative musical decision-making regarding my CD. I was counting on passionate musical individuals to work with me on creating a musical dream of grade A+ songs with awesome musical tracks, balanced perfectly by my blessed vocals.

Walking around the corner to my car and then driving south out of Los Angeles, I prayed and reflected on the day's experiences. By the time I arrived home, every ounce of energy was drained from me. Saying hello and goodnight, I crawled into bed, still pondering who those two nice, musical guys were.

The following day, I had a voice-over showcase, which was the end to another class which had been a nerve-wracking but fun learning experience. These voice-over classes were getting me out of my box and thinking quickly on my feet. The focus of voice-over is strictly on the vocal production and nothing about who looks the best. These classes were only igniting my love for expressing myself passionately through singing.

Over the next three weeks I practiced singing, "Let Go." The first week, I taught my youngest son's third grade class music. Elementary school music classes had been cut drastically and the teacher, Mrs. Price, was happy to have me be musical with the children. We all had shakers and were clapping rhythms. I asked them questions about music and their taste in music. Shyly, they would respond very coyly, looking interested in what I was saying to them about being musical. I learned as much as they did that day, and Brycer was pleased to hear his mom sing for his class. The weeks flew by, and then finally Rue agreed it was time and I was ready to record the song. I was solid on the specific arrangement of "Let Go."

Nervously, I drove to Hollywood giggling out loud to myself. Record in Hollywood? Me? Then I would reflect on the location above a pizza joint in a loft studio with nice wood floors. It was downright funny to me. The dream of a small child to record in Hollywood was coming alive, but a bit differently than I had pictured it.

It wasn't long after I arrived that Christian came. I had brought some coffee as another expression of my appreciation and to show who "Ln" is inside. Lauren told me that Christian would be engineering me. I stood by nervously, waiting to sing while the track was brought up on the computer and mixed for a few moments. These minutes to me were like eternity, but I tried to act relaxed. I went into the bathroom to say a prayer and have a moment of peace.

Finally, Christian said, "Into the closet." This closet had been turned into a soundproof area with thick padding and a microphone. I had previously seen Candace recording vocals from in the closet and now today it was my turn.

I turned off my cell phone but had it in my pocket. Somehow, the idea of being in a soundproof medium-sized closet with a closed door scared me. Caution told me to keep the cell phone in case these men I hardly knew turned in an evil direction. Call it paranoia. I called it making good sense as a woman or person among strangers.

Christian had me speak to test the microphone level against the music until I felt it sounded right in the headphones and it was good for his recording purposes too. Then Christian sensed my apprehension and casually told me, "Just sing the song through all the way to warm up."

The music started and I began to sing. The pain of my life melted off with each phrase of the song. Almost at the ending, Christian stopped me and said, "Yes Ma'am! You are letting go and it sounds great." Lauren told me how professional I sounded and what a pleasure it was to work with a vocalist who comes in knowing what they are doing vocally. I was thankful they didn't kick me out, and relieved to be on track and recording, even if it was in a closet.

Line by line, Christian had me sing several times as he took me down the path of a top recording session. The closet became warm at one point, and I was offered water and then encouraged to take a break about two-thirds of the way through recording. Coming out of the closet, I was surprised in an eerie way to see some guy sitting on the couch. I requested not to have anyone present except Christian (beside Lauren himself), and this stranger looking at me was creating an uncomfortable feeling. I had a strong sense of wanting my privacy while recording, or at least until getting to know who was working with me and if they were truly trustworthy.

I was introduced to this tall, big male as the next-door neighbor. I was polite, but inside, my feelings were of disappointment for my wishes not being respected. I had wanted to have total privacy while recording with only Christian and Lauren there. I knew there would be a time and a place to express myself, but not while in session, recording. I had paid to be recorded singing my best and only this idea was what mattered to me. I didn't want to feel "on display" as an artist yet.

I had never been recorded like this before, line-by-line. It made sense. This is the more professional way. Vocals are recorded, then cut and pasted until the best of the best is there. Even if singing the song through correctly is possible, this makes it easier on the vocalist.

It felt foreign at first, but Christian's "Yes Ma'am" helped to assure me he was a respectful, hardworking, sincere person, and that he was trying to help get the best recording from me. At one point, I could hear Lauren talking on his cell phone close outside the closet, telling someone of my singing talent and my wide range. Alone in the closet, I was very aware of the process of recording in Hollywood, wow! Funny, I never pictured it like this.

The process took a couple hours, with time out of the closet to give Lauren a chance to make up the interlude near the ending. There was a glitch in the lyrics where the phrasing was not good enough or not making as much sense as it could. Soon, Lauren brainstormed and created the lyric lines. In the end, we three thought it was a great addition to the song. Soon, I was done with the environment of a recording session, and happy with my recorded singing outcome. I was impressed with the high level of musical creativity these two had shown me.

After it was over, I was there for a little while and then Lauren walked me out. He told me I had done a great job. I thanked him and parted ways to drive the hour back home. Soon, I was safe back in my neighborhood and excited to tell my children of my vocal recording session.

Brycer asked me, "Are you a star yet?" When I told him I wasn't yet, he reassured me, "Don't worry. You will be if you just keep trying, keep singing."

Two days passed with me feeling relieved. I was glowing in the accomplishment of a successful recording. Then on the third day, my anxiety started to build about not having any copy of the recording. The memories of crooked Egg Dolly crept in on my thoughts until I lay in the dark that night, struggling with my choices. Had I done the right thing in trusting Christian and Lauren, or was this going to end up with them denying it was me singing on the recording? It was Lauren's song, so the copyrights were not mine, but the voice singing was. Tears ran down my cheeks as I wept silently; I tossed and turned early in the evening, alone in bed. What was I to do and how long until I would have the recording or know the answer to my bigger question, were they honest musicians and producers?

After several hours of this self-torment, I had to find a release for my emotional pain. The memories of the sexual abuser were haunting me, too. That was the final straw for me. I picked up the phone and called Lauren and left a message. Soon, he responded and was upset with my impatience. I tried to explain my deep anxiety and anguish. I felt humiliated that I wasn't able to be braver. As Lauren spoke louder and more firmly to me, I grew more afraid. Eventually, I stood up for myself and calmly told him that it was the abuse memories, and he was not the problem; the ugly memories were. I said, "I know I can sing, but please try to understand that I was sexually abused and it's causing me anxiety, so can you help me?" I was giving it one last chance to express my dilemma to Lauren.

Suddenly, he switched his confused irritated voice to the most loving, compassionate, and supportive tone possible. He soon agreed to have me come up in a few more days to pick up a rough mix, asking if it would be possible for me to relax if I knew that on Thursday I could have it. He was genuinely concerned and said that if it had to be sooner, he was willing to accommodate my weakened spirit. This impressed me greatly, and I told him thanks so much and that would be just great.

We hung up the phone February 23rd, and I rolled once again onto my side and wept for almost an hour, as the pain of being abused as a child, and again by Mr. Dolly, flowed out like water through a broken dam. Eventually, my crying eased. I dried my face and went to tell my husband and sons the good news. On Thursday, February 26th, my first professional vocal recording would be safely playing in my home. Having this knowledge was such a huge comfort to me. Drained completely, I went to sleep early that night.

Three days later, I was standing outside the green door again on Melrose Boulevard with the Italian smell of the pizza place floating by me. I called Lauren, who warned me he was just going to run down to hand it to me as he had a studio recording in session. Gratefully, I took the CD and thanked him for understanding my stressful situation. I remarked that it was humiliating to me, but he was gentle, saying the way I sing is healing and for me not to forget that part of me. We parted ways, with him back inside the green door and me briskly walking to my car. My body trembled as I put the CD in the car player. From the start of the song, I began to cry as "Let Go" played. The prayers of thanks to God were endless and for my producer and his son, too. I was amazed by lyrics of the song and the voice singing them. How could it be me with this remarkable instrumentation and melody?

I was almost to the freeway when my urge to leave a "thank you" message for Lauren overcame me. Now, I was much more confident that he was the right person for me to trust with my singing talent. The fears were melting away in me, layer by layer. Christian was a producer I could have faith in and believe that he had my best intentions as a musically talented, gifted human being. My musical ship was sailing toward the end of a journey, with my singing more golden than ever. Soon, a smile of pure happiness grew bigger upon my face the more miles I drove away. Over and over I played this first recording. It was a miracle of peace to me.

I had put off starting to write the book, which was the other big piece to the puzzle of my life. Lauren had handed the book idea to me in the studio the first day we talked about my career. I pledged today that I would write something. It was February 27th, 2004, almost one week after recording the first song, "Let Go." That day went by with no writing, so I told myself, tonight is the night there would be no sleep until something in writing was started. I felt like I was in college again, when you stay up late to cram and get something done, only I knew this would be the start of my life story in a self-help format. It would be the project of a lifetime: It would be writing my autobiography where each chapter would reflect and fit a song. For several hours I procrastinated, checking emails, surfing every subject possible on the Internet. How to write? How to make sense of my life? How to help others? I spent hours of soul searching and reflecting upon my passion to sing and life at forty-seven.

At 3:30 a.m., February 28th, 2004, I had grown extremely tired and told myself that there is to be no sleep until you write a sentence. I thought of my producer's daughter, Candace's spunk and the feistiness she had shown me. Something similar that was in me back when I was in my early twenties but is now long forgotten. I had been a frightened college girl who began to study and discover how not to be inhibited to sing. I hit on the right catalyst to start the book with Candace in mind, as if it was her I was talking to instead of my computer, and I began to write an introduction.

Next, I remembered what Lauren had said about writing an outline. First, I wrote one sentence thinking bedtime would come next, but then another sentence came and another. Clearly I was speaking to Candace, another much younger musical spirited person with an amazing voice too, who I thought surely would understand my right to express myself no matter that I was a female. The sentences came running out of my head in a fast and furious way, as if this story had been pent up in me for far too long.

Exhausted, I finally hit the end of writing and saw it was almost 4:30 a.m. Wow, me writing a book. My college writing Professor, Frank Blume, would be proud. I was going against all the odds of being capable of writing a book because of my lack of ability to write correctly in a flowing manner. I prayed what he told me in front of the college Master's graduation committee would come true and I would write a best seller. Not for the fame, but for explaining to millions of people why singing is a healing experience we all need to do on some regular level. I had opened the door that had been closed tightly in me for decades, and this time I would be fighting within myself to stay on track until whatever was burning inside me was out. This was my calling, my mission in life, something no one else was meant to do but me. Little old me fell quickly asleep, waking up to remember the accomplishment the night before and reading with interest to see that it wasn't half bad. There was sense on the page, thank God. I emailed producer Lauren a copy for his feedback.

Checking my email, I read this from my new producer. My eyes could not believe what they read.

"02/28/04: I had no idea that your natural writing style was so engaging. You have an amazing gift of communicating in a valid understandable way while making the reader feel as if they are a friend. I will tell you that the task of writing a book has escaped many a highly intelligent group of educated people, but NOT YOU!!!!!!!! If the book stands up to this opening, you are on the way to a milestone of personal expression and healing for others that have the pleasure of you're influence. Great job!!!!!! Lauren"

"Thank you God! He likes it! He enjoyed my writing? I can write? WOW," I said, talking out loud to myself in total shock. Soon, visiting Rue, I read my story's introduction as she listened. I was back at home when she called to say, "You are a great writer!" I agreed it had been too long since writing lyrics, and it was time that happened again. She corrected me, saying, "You are great at lyric writing, but Ellen you are a great book writer, too. The writing you read to me is still within me and I'm thinking over what all you said." I told her of reading Lauren's email and now believed his words more after hearing hers, too. It was amazing to me that my writing was getting my point across.

The month of March, 2004, marked over seven years after my husband's fall accident. I was studying voice-over classes in teleprompting (among other subjects) as well as mothering my two sons. I had to get Kyguy's eyes checked and attend the elementary school volunteer tea. I was still going to see Dr. Rubel for counseling every other week, determined not to stop until my singing had found its rightful home.

Once a week, I would meet girlfriends to chat, dance, and enjoy the three-piece band. I also became friends (or so I hoped) with these three musicians. At that point, I was still naïve about how certain professional, small time musicians were more into playing something else besides their musical instruments. All I knew was the music healed my spirit to go on with my life, of working in an office and heading toward my musical dreams. I still greatly missed the nights playing with Xavi, Susi, Frances, the Tooth Brothers, David, and an assortment of musicians. Everyone was a uniquely musically spirited person at Lord Tiger Studio. Hopefully, listening to this three-piece band would take away the emptiness felt since the Lord Tiger disbanded. The great memories were fading away, leaving a musical void in my life.

In March, around the thirteenth, I went to Lauren's Vision Studio to meet with the bass player from the band. The music track instrumentation for the second song, "Crystal Clear," the song James Hamilton had said was mine to record a year and a half prior, was uniquely updated, and sounded beautiful. I had hopes the singer in the band would sing the duet with me, as he had a glorious vocal range. The bass player from the band had agreed to work in the studio on the song. I insisted on paying him top dollar for recording on the CD. I wanted to get his opinion of my producers, thinking as he had more experience in the music business.

What I know more than anything now is: Don't ask any musician what he thinks of another because nine times or more out of ten, they are too insecure to give you the truth. They only want you to worship the ground they walk on and throw money at them, which is not what I am about. Paul, a very young but experienced musician, gave me that piece of advice. I instead choose to appreciate the gifts all people have been given, musical or otherwise.

By the time the bass player left, both of my producers were warning me about who I was hanging around with, which puzzled me. In the end, I learned the hard way, if some guy's nickname is, "Button," it means he supplies people with a drug called "peyote buttons." My mistake was in not trusting my producer's judgment at the time. After all, I had listened to the three guys playing music weekly for a year. It's hard to admit to myself how evil a person can sometimes be. I know Dr. Rubel is right. It is more about the evil person than about me. I tend to see the good in people, while they try to manipulate others for their own sick satisfaction.

After the bass for "Crystal Clear" was recorded, the bass player left and Christian took a break to go get something to eat. Lauren and I talked about music and the seedy side of the business, along with other details or questions I had. He was always very professional in guiding my project. He helped me to look at the process I was involved in with my music and writing my autobiographical self-help book too.

Eventually, Christian came back to the studio, having cooled off from the strange bass player from whom he picked up bad vibes. I felt bad and confused but didn't let it affect my work with Lauren and Christian. I was grateful Christian was fine with me and working together in the studio, only asking for me not to bring the guy in again. I made a note of it and left it at that. It took a while before Christian, Lauren, and I were creating the lyric to my theme song. "Come on and Sing," or "Sing Song," as it would be often referred to as. Then we began to brainstorm, writing the words to "Come On and Sing," anchoring this with my hook. Lauren was sitting in the computer chair writing down what ideas were talked about, I was resting on one couch, and Christian was sitting on my left on another couch.

Initially, if I were not receptive to his ideas, Lauren would speak more with Christian instead of me. Christian was clearly the negotiator between the three of us. If there was a word or idea I felt strongly about, Christian was the one who would hear what came out of my mouth. He would then express to his father this idea or word, until he understood the lyrics I had already sketched out in writing about why everyone should sing. I was a bit anxious at first to show my phrases. Lauren's attention caught onto one phrase, saying, "That's the best hook right there, 'Come on and sing,'" he boldly stated.

We talked about what type of feel I wanted in the song and with the words. It had been the start of dusk outside by the time the three of us started hammering out the lyrics, step by step. The process of creating those words for this song was funny to me. Lauren would talk with me about ideas and then say a phrase, and I would write it into the lyrics. Sometimes, Christian came up with something, which Lauren and I would agree was the right thing.

I was in Heaven, working as a collaborator with two very musically talented and gifted people. This was an amazing group project and before too long, there it was, like a puzzle put together beautifully. Lauren gave me a scratched-out version of the lyrics. We agreed to share rights for the lyrics three ways, and the musical loop Christian had played me the first time I met him would be the musical track.

Monday, Christian told me, the music would be ready for pick up. Again, I walked out of the loft and down the steep stairs to leave through the green magical door. I was now feeling safer in the area to make my way to the street around the corner. I started to drive home, feeling happier than I dreamed possible. I called again to say "Thank-you!" as I made my way back south by way of the freeway maze. I was extremely exhilarated by the incredible process of being a part of making up lyrics and guiding my musical creation of a song with true professionals. I didn't know life could be this good. I was still pondering, who were those two guys?

Monday, I went back up to Hollywood, taking a varying selection of groceries for a gift to the two guys who were making my wildest dreams come true with theme song creations tailored to me. In a short time, I was there and had the music track to "Sing Song" and was driving home playing the music instrumentation in the car, giggling away. Again, I called while driving away to thank them for the great work they were doing for me. This music was like a miracle to me. "Come on and Sing." The song, to me, had a perfect melody and was very inspiring.

On 4 March 19th, 2004, I went up to Hollywood to the studio. Candace opened the green door and it surprised me that her hair color was now black instead of blond. Her lovely blue eyes stood out and her spirit glowed. Candace had been the one who helped calm my nerves in the initial meeting at the studio loft. Her visiting Los Angeles for me was a great treat and time to give thanks to her. I brought a humble little gift for her and Christian, too. I was celebrating making it this far with my music. I knew that "studio rats" (people who work in music studios) usually love food because they often lose track of time without eating anything. I had several bags of food for fun and a musical surprise gift-wrapped in an oversized box for Lauren, her dad.

The day was fun. Candace recorded her back-up part for "Sing Song." I loved listening and watching her and Christian working together as a team. The singing was incredible and the two of them worked well together. I soaked up everything to learn how better to do my part of recording in the future. I didn't have to record anything. I was only there to be a part of the studio. Memories of Lord Tiger Studio days happily floated in and out of my mind.

At one point, Greg was mixing "Let Go" with Lauren, who asked me to watch. It was obvious that Greg, who I had met when he witnessed the signing of the official papers, was very good at the computer music mixing and mastering, an art unto itself. He was a very polite, slightly soft-toned young man who impressed me by his nature.

There was only one brief moment when my anxiety crept up, which was when Lauren asked me if it was okay if he walked to the store nearby for something. Christian and Candace were in the bedroom catching up as siblings can do. I found myself in the living room with my song playing over and over as Greg fine-tuned the musical mix. Soon, different young males that were Christian's friends, including Tron, showed up until there were quite a few hanging around in the studio. As I sat stiffly on the side of one couch, these several young men of various sizes all spoke in the latest hip slang words. They said phrases like "off the hook," or "hinges," "that's sick" (something is really great), "w'sup" (hello greeting), "we're chillin" (relaxing), etc. I began to realize it wasn't so much as any gang talk as just young people creating their own lingo. It was easy to relate to them, because when I was young, "cool" began to mean something besides just temperature.

Occasionally, one would look my way questioning. "Is that you singing?" Shyly and very self-consciously, I would reply the truth, "Yes." At one point, several of them looked at me and one another repeating, "She's sings sick." I thought they didn't like my singing, and even agreed with one of them that not everyone will like my singing I know. They all seemed puzzled by my expression and then Greg explained to me that sick is a term for something is awesome. I sat trying not to look foolish and smiled. They had always been acknowledging that it was great vocal work. I was fascinated by their very clever speech expressions, and hip terminology. For one brief moment, the number of males in the room with me, the only female, was just a bit scary. Then I settled down to realize this was safe territory with Christian and Candace close by and with Greg, whom I knew as always polite.

The looks on these young men toward me were of high regard for a person who can sing. I was singing, and it was sounding great with the awesome musical background. I had listened to the song for weeks and Rue had heard it, but this was the first group of people who were hearing it and giving me their reactions. Then Lauren came bounding in the door, asking how everything was. I smiled like the Cheshire cat, content. I ended up staying far later than I ever intended to. The hours flew by and finally, I had to insist on leaving for home, giving everyone a hug and thanks. This was a family of musical people and I felt welcome among everyone, which was an amazing moment in my life after so many times of feeling not worthy of being part of some group.

Days later, sad news came. My Aunt Sally had passed away after a crippling and hard fight with lymphoma cancer. She was the aunt with a fiery attitude to match her bright red hair. She was the scariest aunt I had growing up, but in the last years of her life the hard shell that kept me distant had melted. The last time I saw her was at a family picnic where, sitting frail in a wheelchair, she asked me gently, "How is your music coming? You should be singing, you know?"

I shared with her my latest and the new producers to work with. She encouraged me greatly over and over. She told me point blank, "Don't let anyone stop you from singing, because you have talent and that comes only from one person: God." She made me promise to go forward until I make people listen to me sing. We agreed that the best thing in life is doing something for charity. Aunt Sally had dedicated her life to raising five children and volunteering for charity work.

The day I heard she had passed away to Heaven was sad for me. I worried about Uncle Jimmy, who was now suddenly done with being a caregiver. The next day, I worked myself too hard lifting heavy boxes at work until I pulled my leg muscle terribly and had to limp to my car. Driving home, Lauren called, returning my call to him. I had horrible pain in my hip that was shooting down my right leg. My words to him were sarcastic and not nice, "Don't tell me this is Lauren." He went off on me, as I deserved until I explained the situation with my aunt's passing and my getting injured. He settled down and agreed to talk at a better time. In increasing pain, I desperately worked to drive home and crawl in bed, until the next morning, when the service was to begin.

Her memorial service at the grave site was beautiful, with each of my cousins and my Uncle Jimmy releasing birds to soar as I pictured my fiery aunt in Heaven, no longer bound by any physical disabilities. There was a sad peace. My younger brother Haines stood next to me as I cried for the loss of so many others in my life. I remembered what my Aunt Sally had made me promise and said prayers for her.

After a lovely luncheon, there was a church service. Haines had gone back to work, but I was there to represent my side of the family. I wasn't very close to my Aunt Sally until that last picnic, but I knew the significance of staying with my cousins and uncle. I sat with my father's, youngest sister, Aunt Carol, her husband, Uncle Jess, and youngest daughter, Robin. The church seemed huge, with a handful of people sprinkled in it.

The minister said anyone could go up front to speak about my aunt. Slowly, her children and their spouses went up to speak. Sitting in the church pew a moment came when I said, "I have to go!" My youngest cousin, Robin, thought I meant to leave the church; instead I went to the front and soon it was my turn to walk the steps up to the glorious front of this magnificent church. I knew for my family there must be something said about this woman, my Aunt Sally, who, with her body failing, was still holding strong to inspire others to show their strength and be a lion unto the world for goodness as she had done for me months previously. Whatever I said was spontaneous, and I sang a bit of the song sung decades before at my youngest cousin Keifer's funeral, "In This Place," by Robin Trower. Tears ran down my cheeks as I shivered, walking back to the pew to sit again, praying for peace inside the glorious, beautiful, church. It was a longer day than I expected, but it will live with me on the journey for a day that was as meaningful or reflective as any other will ever be.

The next time at the studio in Hollywood was three weeks later on a Saturday, April 10. I brought gifts of food as a way of saying an extra thank you in advance of the recording session. I had brought some Florida crab claws and shrimp, which Lauren cooked up for Greg, Christian, and I when he showed up. I was celebrating the joy of my music and being far away from the medical world or the intense life of being a caregiver. To me, it was just showing who I am, "a very kind and generous woman," as Dr. Rubel had clearly stated to me on several occasions in therapy. To me, I see a need and it is natural to attempt to fill it or help others. That makes me feel at peace, calm, happy, and worthy of being alive. Besides, I now knew the price I was paying at this studio was very reasonable for the superior quality work.

This was the first time I really started to get to know who this guy "Greg" was. He was very bright and pleasant to speak with. I found Greg to be one of the nicest people to communicate with on any level. He understood my passion for music, as well as other subjects we discussed, in an easy open way. He had a gentle, focused, and calm spirit. It was very refreshing that a younger person was able to hold a two-way conversation.

It wasn't long before Christian showed up. First, I asked if it would be possible for him to take a listen to my own song, "Inside My Heart," and to make a music track to it for the third song. Christian responded that he would be capable of making a hot music track to anything I wanted.

This time, I told Christian the music track, of "Crystal Clear" was difficult for me. I had called Christian while working on my vocal arrangement with Rue because we both had a heck of a time figuring out the melody lines of where the verses were and the chorus was. The musical track was beautiful, but much different instrumentally, and it was throwing me off. I felt lost in the dark with no walls. There were no easy musical marking or instruments playing where I could sing and understand mentally where in the sound I was. It was a lovely musical track creation, but I felt completely inadequate. It had taken me twice-a-week sessions working with Rue before I could get any handle on passionately singing the song. At last I went to record, trusting that Christian and Lauren would help me, as they are both singers and believe in the contract we had signed, saying if I did not record to my liking it was to be redone.

Again, I was back in the vocal booth, which was a soundproof closet, a space of about three feet by three feet. Finally, Christian started singing along to the track. I was extremely nervous in the closet with the headphones on. I prayed hard and told myself, "You do this one for James, your guardian angel, who believes in you and to who God gave the talent to write this awesome song."

Slowly, phrase by phrase, painstakingly with Christian saying, "Yes Ma'am" over and over, we inched through the song. When I took a break to get a drink of water, I was almost in tears. Never had singing been so hard for me to accomplish in my whole life, but the vocals coming out of me were fine.

Lauren appeared in the kitchen and asked how I was doing. The look on my face must have said a thousand words, because I was struggling so hard to not walk out of the studio, cry, and give up. Lauren was distracted, looking for his missing camera and something else, which only added to the pressure of my feeling lost in the music track. I felt as if a whale called "music" was swallowing my essence. There was no feeling of riding a wave, but of being bounced around helplessly in the whitewater of the hurricane's surf. If I live to be hundred, I hope to never feel that way singing ever again. It was beautiful music, with the scariest sense that something was very wrong within me.

Back in the soundproof room, Christian sensed my pain and spoke even more encouragingly to me. Tears ran down my cheeks as I tried to hug myself and comfort the awful way I felt. There was no room for defeat, which was not an option. If there is one thing I am capable of doing, it is singing; and if that leaves me, then who will I be or what can I do?

Slowly, with Christian's amazing patience, we persevered through the song. The high notes came and the will to fight came back to me. I was mad, and feeling more focused to let out what this painful thing to sing was within my deepest being. Christian's "Yes Ma'am" was the only thing I heard. I imagined James Hamilton (my friend, and the writer of the song) held me together while recording alone in the tiny closet, in which Christian had duck-taped the lyrics to the door jam. I eventually figured out that if I put my hands up to the low shelf above my head, gently pressing as I sang, this helped by distracting me from outside thoughts. I was there singing, at one with the music. Often, Christian would sing the phrase then sing with me and then have me record. The sweetest moment was when Christian said, "That's it! Yes Ma'am! You are Crystal Clear!"

I was finished with a song I'm proud to have recorded on April 10th, 2004, three days before Kyguy turned sixteen. I think giving birth to him was easier than giving birth to this song. I learned that sometimes it takes a few tears to record an awesome song along with a Florida-boy saying, "Yes Ma'am."

I was irritated by Lauren's distraction, looking for missing and apparently stolen items from his loft. Even as hard as I tried to understand, it felt like the contract we signed and his word to always be in the studio were not being carried out. It was just the whole event that was frustrating to me. I didn't come to record often and should have left when he realized things were stolen. He needed time to search for them, and looking back now, I know that leaving would have been better than going ahead. It was partly because of the huge pressure I felt to do the music business the correct way and not be taken advantage of again. Not knowing Christian very well with his being so young, it had made me leery just having his input, which I understand now was truly wonderful during a difficult recording session. That day, I started to feel that Christian was a dream to work with during recording. He was compassionate toward me in an unthreatening way, which enhanced my ability to focus on singing passionately.

After recording, I went to see my friend Deanna and her band, Savage City, who were playing in Beverly Hills. I asked Lauren to come to hear her, wanting to record a three-chick empowerment song along with Candace. One of my dreams would be to record with two other vocally rocking chicks a song with the power, just like Helen Reddy had in the song, "I Am Woman." Nothing against males, but using music and strong, feminine girl power to spread the message to wake up and be you, empowering other females, just makes sense and feels right to me. Don't let anyone put you down because you are a girl or a woman, young or old.

I was waiting a long time for Lauren to show up and was about to give up on his coming. The place had a rustic look to it with the typical long wooden bar. He showed up, bringing along a couple of young friends. They were standing in the front opposite end of the long room where I had paid for two people's cover charge. I had told Lauren of this, but he had to stop to pay the third person and ended up at the front of the bar. So I thought he was wanting to stay with his friends and that we would talk later about Deanna's vocals.

I was sitting in a booth up front in the middle of the room, enjoying Deanna's singing and her nine-piece band with an awesome brass instrument sound. The next thing I knew, Lauren walked by with his two lady friends, searching for a place. One of the ladies recognized me and I politely waved, smiling. She must have told Lauren while I was distracted back to Deanna's incredibly fun singing. Quickly, there was Lauren sitting beside me, and the two ladies sat across from me momentarily until they decided to move to the booth across the short aisle for a better view of the band.

It was very hard to hear with the brass section playing close in front. When the song ended, Lauren and I would speak about my idea to record with Deanna. Soon, Deanna took a break and came to meet my producer. She sat down across from us and we three spoke about music. Lauren appreciated the several great brass instruments in the band, as well as the others, and her singing too. Then Cy, the manger of the band, came to meet Lauren. She eventually excused herself to go socialize with others who were there to hear the band.

It was during this band break that I spoke to Lauren about wanting to record a cover song. He agreed, but was unable to think of just the right one. I had been certain for years that one cover needed to be redone, as was the style in the music world. Nervous to trust anyone at that moment, I made Lauren promise to only let me record the song and no one else. He seemed not to be taking me seriously until I told him this song would be great redone and I want to sing it. Finally, the band was playing and I had to speak directly into his ear for the conversation to continue. I told him the song was Johnny Rivers' "Secret Agent Man." He threw his head back with a huge smile remarking happily, "Yes I would love to redo that song with you singing it!" He looked at me with shock that I, little old me, could come up with the idea that this song was perfect to update and have a female singing it. I just shook my head shyly and said, "Perfect, isn't it?" He looked grinning at me saying, "Yes, it's yours! I won't tell anyone but Christian. What a great idea."

Soon, he excused himself to switch seats to the booth across the small aisle and sat with his young lady friends. I had accomplished my mission for him to hear Deanna, who someday, I will sing a song with and to tell him the cover song on my project. It fit perfectly with my life story of speaking with an FBI agent. These are some of the people who put their lives on the line to protect our country every day, secret agent men and women.

The next band break, Lauren said goodnight and left with his friends. Soon after, I left too and became lost on the drive home, which put me on the most bizarre way home from Beverly Hills possible. I wasn't even familiar with where Beverly Hills was, but eventually I did arrive back to my hometown. I made it home thinking of the thrill of hearing the band Savage City. I was also relieved to have another song recorded: "Crystal Clear," written by James Hamilton.

The following week was an upheaval between Lauren and me. It had turned that out one of his stolen things was something I had lent him. This was unsettling to me. I had only known him four months, given him a lot of money, and didn't honestly know what to think about this latest development. I didn't want to be taken advantage of by anyone, especially another male or musician. We both tried hard not to get too mad with each other, but at times it was border-line for both of us.

After ending the lengthy phone conservation with Lauren, I prayed for less anxiety in the future. Something in my gut was again saying to trust Lauren and his son Christian, the twenty-three year old kid, who was actually an impressive young man. The young person who had asked me when we first met, "Are you spiritual?" This question kept popping up in my head. If I was spiritual, then trusting these two gifted and talented spiritual people might be the right solution to a problem beyond Lauren's control. Property was important, but the lives of people and trust of them must weigh in somewhere too.

I stayed true to my feelings, as Rubel had encouraged me in therapy to do with speaking to anyone. I told Lauren how disappointed and concerned I felt not to have his full attention while recording. It was very hard to stay strong and stand up to him, but thoughts of negotiating as a child with my own father helped me to hold my own in this music business world. Rue encouraged me. He was the one that signed the contract, and Lauren is the one that needs to give you one hundred percent of his attention when you record. He is award-winning and that is what you paid for, want, need, and deserve. Bit by bit over the phone, we exchanged our feelings about the project, the recording session, and my lost mini dat player. Over and over to myself I would say, "Am I spiritual?" I was glad to know Lauren could not see the tears falling from my eyes. We settled the difficulties that arose from the last recording session and still had a mutual respect between us as music professionals.

Afterwards, I wrote Candace, who responded with her super girl power, "4/29/04 You say what you gotta say girl!!! love, Candace."

All my life, the fear of hurting others was weighing so heavy on me, I was usually too afraid to say what was on my mind. Slowly, this was falling away from the relationship I had with both Lauren and Christian. I knew that for this to work and for my music to be what was best for me, this had to happen. It was almost painful for me to speak up to these strong, outspoken southern Florida boys, but I pushed hard ahead to have my say, too.

By the end of April, I had a track of my original song, "Inside My Heart," which was recorded first onto a cassette after I made it up while taking a shower. The second time, it was recorded with Xavi building a music track. The third time was with A+, my choir director, playing a grand piano in a studio. Now there was a new, updated musical track Christian had created that sounded beautiful. The lyrics this time would be pared down to fit the music, as Christian had built the music track shorter in length by two verses. This time, the lyrics jelled into a beautiful expression of what I heard singing in the shower to begin with, "Inside My Heart." Rue worked joyfully with me to create what we both thought were great lyrics, condensed to an amazingly lovely version of my melody.

I was pushing forward and writing the third chapter. I was overwhelmed by the amount I had to write, but happy to be able to put something on the computer screen.

This was an email sent to me on 05-11-04, after writing to Lauren about the music and book writing: "Funny how things come back around. I have seen you find your wings in the last few weeks and it is fun to watch you find empowerment through the talents that God has given to you. This project is a journey that will make a difference in the lives of others. The difference will be communicated through the one that has taken the journey. I have read the first half of the book and was interrupted by my workload. I will finish it soon and give you my thoughts. I have had to distance myself from those people who are unhealthy or want to cause problems in my life. I do not understand why some people want to live in a world of unkind intentions. I know you have had that happen as well, and I am glad to know that you are allowing yourself the freedom to do the same. You are a great person and should surround yourself with those that are worthy to be your friend. I am honored to have the opportunity to help you accomplish this project and will do the very best job I can. God Bless, Lauren"

On Saturday, May 22nd, 2004, I went up to the Bodi Tree Book store on Melrose Boulevard to research and buy books on music's healing ability. It had been almost three decades since visiting the cutting-edge, innovative, spiritual bookstore. It had expanded greatly in inventory and space. I was mesmerized the moment I entered the unusual bookstore, eventually finding my favorite area related to music. I sat down to sort through all the books, until narrowing down my search to the several I would purchase.

I left to find my way to where Christian and his band were to play at a festival. I was supposed to record this Saturday, but he had the opportunity to play at a festival, so we agreed to reschedule. I went, excited to see him sing with his band and wondering what his musical spirit in full force would be like to experience. It was a bit of a drive to find the event held at Jackie Robinson Stadium in Rancho Cienega Park. Having never been to this type of festival, I was intimated, but there was nothing that was going to stop me from the experience of something new. The Malcolm X festival was intriguing and interesting with lots of nice, friendly, happy people. I stood out with my light colored skin, but I thought of President Lincoln and knew there were friends here in my midst. The parking lot attendants were well-behaved, nice gentlemen.

As I walked up to the festival, I saw beautiful women decked out in African-looking draped dresses with their sweet, adorable children. I felt proud to be an American with the shades of people from all walks of life everywhere, and proud to be able to have the free will to attend a festival unlike any I had attended before. The first speaker I passed was on a microphone saying some harsh words about our government and the lack of help by some types of people of certain ancestry like myself. I shook my head "yes" because there was truth in the statement, but not necessarily having anything to do with my decision-making. A man working the festival entrance smiled toward me, saying, "Welcome." That meant a lot to me as I thought about one of my heroes, Martin Luther King, and his belief in unity of all people.

I struggled to find Christian and Lauren. I ended up by mistake at the "kiddy rides" area that was now shut down after a long hot day. Sunset was coming soon. Then I asked a gentleman at a booth for directions who pointed to a stage explaining how to get there. The booths of colorful things for sale impressed me and I longed to have more time to spend at them, but I hurried to make sure not to miss

Christian's performance. Seeing the people leaving, it was obvious that the festival was winding down after a long and glorious day.

On the grass side where the stage was, hundreds of chairs were in rows. The band playing was doing a great job with reggae style music. It was simple to understand the music, which all day long had to have been wonderful. I regretted not coming earlier. I caught a glimpse of Christian and then Lauren behind the stage by the black hummer. Soon I had spotted Natalie, Christian's girlfriend, and her mother Michelle up in the front row. I was too shy to sit by them. I only wanted to steal a listen of Christian doing his thing on a stage. This to me would tell me more about him than anything else. I was almost holding my breath with excitement waiting to observe Christian's musical spirit shining full force toward an audience. It was incredible to finally be able to hear the one recording me sing on a stage.

I was having a hard time sitting down. To me, the music makes me feel like moving, and with a whole field of grass to stand and dance in place, well, why not? I saw another person doing this so I did too. I clapped as loud as anyone there when the songs ended. Lauren came up to me and said hello for a minute. There was another band and then Christian's. The moment he started to sing, I was greatly impressed. He was very at ease on the stage and his vocals shined forth with a depth of passion like the best professional. The songs and the band playing were awesome too. Each member of the band knew what they were doing and loved their instruments as one. There was only a sprinkling of people left as the dark of night came, but the music was tops.

I danced more and more, loving the music raining down and healing my spirit. There is no better moment for me than great music. This band of young musicians along with Christian singing was professional and the music was very hot sounding. Alive with the music as one, they played on. When they were finished, I walked up to congratulate him on his great music. Lauren and Christian introduced me to the band members, who were all young men. Each one was kind toward me and accepted my difference in skin color as they saw my thrill about their music.

Suddenly, I remembered something I had brought in a cooler to give Christian. I had ordered flower Hawaiian leis to bring into the studio, but because of the festival, the studio for me was cancelled. I had the leis to bring for Christian to show my appreciation of his performance. I ran like a playful kitty across the field to the car, grabbed the lei and hurried backstage to find Christian, praying he wouldn't leave.

Soon, I found him and put the lei over his head, with a wish of luck, I told him what an amazing performer he was. Soon, he came back almost hesitantly to ask if he could give it to Natalie. I told him it would be right for him to give the lei to the one he loves. Then I explained to Christian the reason I gave it to him was for the love of the music he performed today and was creating for me in the studio. Next, he walked over to Natalie, who was sitting in the back seat of a car, while Lauren and I watched. Natalie's mother was sitting in the front seat. Soon Christian was calling me over, stopping me from leaving at that moment. I went to see the beautiful, sweet, petite Natalie sitting in the back seat, and said hello to her. Christian told me to explain what I thought was Hawaiian custom for a lei to be given to a person who then gives it to another they love. After I spoke, Christian said beautiful words to Natalie, placing the lei over her head as Michelle (Natalie's mother) and I looked on.

Christian and Natalie looked so much in love; it was shining in the darkness of the night. I was proud to have been a part of this moment in time. The words Christian said to me before I left will stay with me a lifetime. He said I was like family now and that he was going to do everything possible to help me with my musical dreams and performing career singing. This was a "Kodak moment" and I knew God was working through me to bring peace to all.

Again I scampered to my car and left for the drive back, finding my way out of nowhere to some place called home. The music track for "Inside My Heart" was playing in the car the entire way home. I was proud of having the courage to go somewhere different.

A few days later, I showed up at Rue's, depleted of energy. She quizzed me about what was wrong. It was overwhelming to me to be writing the book, because it meant getting in touch with my traumatic life in the past. Rue tried to encourage me as to how great the idea was with chapter titles of a book matching song titles. Then seeing my unresponsiveness to anything she said, Rue surprised me with, "Well, If I start writing my life story would that help you to go on and keep writing your life story?"

"Yes, because I would love to know and read your life story. You would do that for me?" I said in shock.

"Yes baby, I would if that keeps you writing too," Rue spoke perkily. Soon, Rue and I made the pact to each other to write our life story and stick together as writers of a book encouraging each other. I left that day thinking how great a mentor she has been in my life, always there and inspiring me forward. She was uplifting me to greater heights than ever now.

On May 28th, 2004, I went up to Hollywood and through the magic dark green door to the loft studio. This was wonderful for me to celebrate recording my original song now with a modern updated musical background track, "Inside My Heart." I wanted to celebrate the gift of life this day in a meaningful way. I had decided on bringing flowers. Leis were perfect. They would be something happy and colorful to wear and relax me while recording in the small vocal closet with the beautiful scent of plumeria. The ambience of the smell fit the lovely melody of the song to me. I brought manly leis for Lauren and Christian, too. The sunshine in the window and the flowers uplifted my spirits to sing with more joy than ever. I used my psychology to create an environment to record better than ever in. The scent of plumeria and tuberose was noticeable. The two Florida boys, Christian and Lauren, had never een nor smelled flower leis, having never been to Hawaii. For me, there was magic in the air with the music track playing. I was in heaven on the islands of the South Pacific in my mind's eye.

Driving home, I was still enjoying the scent of Hawaiian flowers around my neck, playing the music track, and thankful for living to see this glorious day in a recording studio. The drive home was long with traffic, but I did not mind a bit.

In June, 2004, I started by seeing Madonna for the first time at the Arrowhead Pond. The seats were far away, but the stage production was a feat to witness and the music delightful. She is an ultimate performer; I admired her as a woman in the entertainment business.

The next meeting at the Vision studio was to get a basic recorded mix with vocals included on a track of the song, "Crystal Clear," along with a rough music instrumental track of the next song, "Secret Agent Man," and mostly to talk about the book. The day was Saturday, the fifth of June. I used the money earned throwing papers and files around at work to pay for my music recordings.

Lauren had insisted I read one book to help me in writing my book. Curiously, I agreed, and he told me it was, Dr. Phil's book, Life Strategies. Since high school, I have loved reading any book on psychology, spiritual growth, autobiographies, self-help, interpersonal relationship issues, and mental health. Human behavior is fascinating to me, as well as animal behavior. It had been years since taking the time to read a psychology-related book, so I looked forward to reading a Dr. Phil's book. He certainly came with high regard according to Oprah, as I had seen him a few times on her show. He seemed interesting from a male's point of reference, often making good common sense of difficult situations. I had not seen his show due to my being a caregiver, when my television watching had screeched to a halt.

The minute I began to read his book, it was a refreshing experience. I took in the information relating it to my life's past and present, also relating everything to singing. His writing was easy to read and enjoyable. As a psychology book goes, Dr. Phil's, was right on target to me. It was filled with good ideas that were expressed in a great format.

The next Saturday afternoon, from 2:00 to 4:00, Lauren and I discussed the book across the street from the studio in a Mexican restaurant. At first, my anxiety was high, wondering what questions about the book Lauren would throw my way. Soon it became clear he was interested in having an intellectual discussion on an easy level, much like I had experienced at Johnston College. There was no right or wrong, only the exchange of thoughts to build a better understanding of Dr. Phil's ideas and writing strategies.

I quickly noticed that Lauren took hold of Dr. Phil's thoughts, man to man. I saw clearer the value in Dr. Phil as a man of depth, reaching others to heighten their levels of awareness regarding their own lives, which intrigued me greatly. Lauren's biggest question was about when the book's climax came. I correctly answered where in the book Dr. Phil had made his strongest point that summed up the book's overall purpose.

Where is the part that shows a direction for the reader to try as an individual and where the tone of the book changes? I saw that moment as three-quarters of the way through the book. Then the book lays out the rest of the time the further netting together of a new way of approaching life strategies. Lauren encouraged me to keep in mind this format (or outlay) of writing to have something similar. I promised to try to understand his point. I drove home, leaving Hollywood behind, with my mind scrambled on the way to write a great book.

June was a moment of truth with my father, unlike any I had in my entire life regarding my passion to sing. He came for a short visit. There was a brief time when it was just he and I in my house.

As I sat at the table with him, we discussed intensely what it was I wanted to do with this music and singing. The pressure on me was greater than all the elephants sitting on you at one time. Finally, with big tears in my eyes, I spoke up saying, "I just want my chance to try and run across the bridge like you did in WWII, to see if I can make it, not to win a silver star like you dad, but instead to let this pain of the talent hidden in me escape and bring me peace of mind."

My father asked, "What if you don't make it across the bridge? Then what?"

"Well, then I can know I tried. And if I make it, then what, dad? God put a gift in me. A talent. Then will you see I sing? I just want to volunteer to try and raise money for charity, with this thing to sing God put in me, your daughter. Will you help me? Or else I will work myself to death to try anyway. This time I am not giving up. You made it across a bridge under gunfire. Do you regret trying?"

With tears about to spill over, I doubted my father would ever understand and empower me in the way he could. I looked up to him, now standing to my right. My dad said something like he could see now that I was never going to stop singing. With big tears in my eyes I looked at him and said, "If I could I would. I would do anything you wanted because I love you dad and you have helped me so much, but I can't stop singing. It's just in my blood. It's just how God made me." He ended with agreeing to think about helping me financially to obtain the resources to pay for my recording a full CD.

When he left, I felt defeated and hopeless that he or anyone in the family could not understand the depth of talent bestowed upon me by God or the pain on a daily basis this had brought to me all my life. I prayed for God to hold me in the palm of his hand and protect me from myself. I felt happy, but torn thinking of all the enthusiastic people who told me that my singing was beautiful over my lifetime. They had said my singing was on a really high level of natural talent that most people are never able to achieve. Yet, my own parents didn't understand this fact at all about their own daughter. My parents would help me with funding to get medical help or to see a counselor, and they had given to charity in large amounts. Unfortunately, they could not see wasting their money on the frivolous act of my singing. To me, any physical pain is much less painful than the emotional turmoil that an artist experiences when their talent is wasting away within them. I felt a failure, yet knew not what more I could do. After my father's visit ended and he left, I cried myself to sleep.

The shock of my life came when a letter arrived the day before my forty-eighth birthday with a check from my dad to empower me on my musical journey. I was so in awe of my start to make it across the bridge. I held this large check $10,000 in my hands, relieved to know my focus could be back on music with writing a book instead of just overworking myself by moving papers around. I called my father to thank him as he downplayed what a beautiful gift he had given me, only reminding me if I don't make it across the bridge, that was fine, too. "Just enjoy the effort to try, and don't expect the music to be played anywhere else, but at your house and say mine, too."

My tears were rolling down my face and bathing me in hope. I had to go to bed and cry again in a state of shock; someone believed in me enough to support me to try to sing. It was the greatest birthday present ever. I will always remember that he reached out to help me sing and record in a professional way.

July came with the next song, "Secret Agent Man," to record at the studio. I showed up looking different. I was dressed up, hair curled, with sunglasses and an aloof attitude like never before, focused on recording the song. I was working to have enough confidence to pull off singing this song. I spoke hardly a word, only thinking in my mind over and over the phrasing of the lyrics as Rue and I had practiced. Soon, the recording session was starting with Christian trying to loosen me up while I stayed in an attitude. I was trying to sing more "edgy," from a place of strong womanly empowerment. The session was over in a short amount of time, and I was out of there.

The song was emailed to me in several days, and when I heard it, I was alarmed at how wrong it sounded. The mix was not right, my vocals were terrible, so it was evident the attitude was not the thing to try. Thankfully, I paid one flat fee, so to record vocals a second time was not going to cost me. I immediately called Rue, telling her it was terrible. She settled me down and we agreed to meet the next day. Meeting together, she listened as I looked at her. I can tell if the music is good or bad and how my singing is by just looking at her. It is like the kid who looks at mom and knows they did right or wrong.

I looked at her and cringed to hear that vocal. The beginning words were not the exactly right ones the original song had, and I did not want to take any liberties with the lyrics. Rue shook her head and said, "No way, you are right to go back in the studio and record this again. It is the pressure of everything going on for you right now, with work, taking care of your children, the family, writing a book, and trying on top of that to record top-level singing."

I called Lauren, who still thought the vocal was perfect. He admitted my appearance in the studio that day was not like me. I was like the dog with its tail between its legs, guilty of wrong-doing. I set up in a week to come to the studio, afraid to wait long for fear of being more and more ashamed of the lousy singing.

The day I showed up to record the song a second time, I came in humbled and shy. I was fearful a poor vocal recording would happen again. Sensing my sadness, Christian spoke softly to me. Both my producers were supportive of my not beating myself up as an artist. I tried something different and learned quickly this was not me. I went in and sang like Christian directed me, which was as simply as I could. The difference was apparent with the brief playbacks. Again Christian said, "Yes Ma'am" and I sang, feeling it was too easy, but he was happy as a clam this time, so I listened to Christian and Lauren's feedback.

It makes no sense to me. The less effort I put into singing (still using my supportive diaphragm or upper stomach muscles), the more deluxe the singing is. How much more of a natural singer could I be? Once again I learned and heard that singing innately, in a simple manner, with your focus on the natural feeling of this physical act, does allow one's singing to sound better. The second mix came days later, and the difference this time with the right words sung in the first line was a relief to my soul. I could breathe again. Peace.

I decide to skip ahead in the book to rewrite my Master's writing paper project as Chapter Five. I looked forward to immersing myself in the updating of information about music and healing. I was excited to add my thoughts gathered over the last twenty-five years to my major paper written long ago. This was an incredible experience to see how cutting-edge I was, and ahead of myself back in my early twenties, deeply interested in singing and music as a huge healing force.

During August this year, I took a road trip with my two sons. I drove all night up the middle of the state of California, and then over toward the coastal area of Northern California to show Brycer and Kyguy some of the oldest and the biggest sequoia trees. Kyguy, Brycer and I spent a magical moment together among these trees where memories of being there many years before with my Aunt Timmy and her grandkids sparkled in my mind. I felt close to her, my angel in Heaven now.

We drove on up through Oregon, until we landed over a country bridge on Toad's farm in the middle of an island on the end of a dirt road. I loved taking my two city kids to get a small taste of small town country living. We picked blackberries to make jam while Brycer was speaking about how amazing it was to go outside and eat from the world around you.

I wanted both of my sons to see the harsh reality of farming life. It has glorious benefits, but work is never-ending. We picked corn, went to the Farmer's Market, made jam, stayed in a little local hotel to get a clean shower, saw the mint being watered with the jumbo sprinkler systems, and visited with the local people my brother knew.

I attempted to explain to my children that because of the Internet, people who live in rural areas had their lives opened up more now than ever before in history. Now anyone with a telephone line could have Internet access. I was amazed at the modernization of lifestyle changes in the rural farming areas because of the Internet influence. Now it was possible in rural places to order things online, or learn about things you would never even knew existed. The attire of people looked more like city dwellers than it had decades before. Since my time studying rural farm life during college, I now saw many changes to the farming community because of the Internet.

Still, the herds of cows and pigs, the cornfields, and seeing land for miles undeveloped with mountains and evergreen trees along the winding highways were the same as decades ago. It was beautiful farming country with scents like mint or dill that can only come from the farmer's world where the land is spacious and one can sing loudly. My favorite part was attending the Farmer's Market, where Toad set up selling his crop from the back of his pickup, using my boys as helpers. I wandered around the Farmer's Market in Eugene, Oregon, loving the few great musicians playing and giving them each a small token of money to help their efforts. I bought a book from an author as well. People who raise crops have something special in their blood. From the salt of the earth, they create food to feed others and themselves.

It was a wonderful trip. Upon leaving the farm with Toad, we went south to visit Aunt Bobbie. She was clear minded, but her eyesight was failing. She spoke to my children with my cousin Michael and his children, too. It was a sad time, departing in the morning with Aunt Bobbie by her back door as my brother and I both realized time had been fleeting, it was passing us all by. That was to be the last time I saw my aunt, but there are a lifetime of memories I shall always carry of her and my Uncle Skeets.

She encouraged me to, "Do what your passion is, and singing is what you love, Ellen. It is your passion and there is nothing wrong with that."

On the entire trip, my poor children had to listen to the music track of the "Sing Song" with Candace singing back up, as I practiced or studied each note. Brycer was quite taken by Candace's vocal, believing she should sing the song, but that it was my theme song.

The three of us drove straight through from Southern Oregon to Southern California, with Kyguy driving a bit since he was well past sixteen. It was a special bonding time for us together. I wanted this moment with my sons because life can turn corners in the future you can't even begin to see. They were both growing up so fast now.

Back home, I went to record "Sing Song," and it went very smoothly. Memories of the great trip to the farm floated through my mind and of me singing to sheep that were looking at me like, what is she doing? I had practiced my "Sing Song" in Toad's farm island meadows, where no matter how loudly I sang or how high, no one would hear except God. The freedom to sing without negative remarks in the open air was such a lovely feeling as always. Now in the studio, the sound of this freedom to sing poured forth fully as Christian captured my vocal. I left rejuvenated, coming back home in peace. There is nothing like a visit to the country to center me to my true deeper spirit.

It would be almost two months before I recorded another song. The next time I went to the studio was to sign an additional paper to correct something discovered by me in the paperwork. Christian played negotiator between his father and me, the client, to make sure the paperwork end of the music business was settled in a positive way for us all. I was hesitating only because of the fear of making too quick of a decision. In the end, I was happy to refocus on writing the end of the third chapter and working on a song Lauren had written years earlier.

It is an anti-suicide song. At first, he was trying to tell me that we could write a new song of the same type. Then I had him read the last part of the chapter about my attempted suicide. He looked at me with compassion and I said the lines to his song, "It happened to me, it can happen to you." He said it would never happen to him, but I told him that is what my cousin David Bellamy had told me after my attempt when visiting my brother in Oregon.

David had been the first person besides my counselor Rubel who really spoke deeply with me late one night. David sat at one end of the kitchen table and me at the other. He wondered if the verbal torment that he, his younger brother Michael, and my older brother Toad, did to me growing up was the reason behind my attempt to take my life. I knew that was not it. I told my cousin I had wanted to sing and David said, "Well sing! Don't give a damn what others think." He spent over an hour telling me how he cared about me and how life is worth living. He explained that he would never attempt suicide. It was a very meaningful moment in my Aunt Bobbie and Uncle Skeet's house, nestled up on a hillside with a forest for a backyard and my older brother sleeping away.

It would be decades later, talking on the phone at Aunt Bobbie's this summer, when my cousin David told me, "You were right. It could happen to me." My cousin had battled alcohol addiction since his Navy days during the Vietnam War. David now admitted over the phone that it did almost happen to him, suicide, a year ago, but he lived through that dark time in his life. He said, "This song you are doing is great, so please do it for me, too."

"You never know where life challenges may take you, and a suicide is not the answer. Commit to love, one day at a time."

I looked at Lauren while I spoke. I was making my case to Lauren again, stressing a lyric line from his song, "Somebody Told Me," and then I pointed to myself saying, "It happened to me." I said seriously to him, "See by the writing how true those words are for me?" He caught my drift and agreed to allow me to use the same track for less money, including his back up.

The biggest surprise and reward for surfing the Internet came in early August. Often between writing the book, I would research sites related to psychology of some type, music, and healing. This had been something I had done for almost a year now. Then one night, I stumbled upon the greatest evidence to support what I had known intuitively and sensed my entire life. Singing is beneficial to one's physical health.

Thanks to all the other supportive, talented musicians whose paths I crossed who helped me to realize that I am musically gifted. May the peace of music and singing always bring great natural healing to you every day.

Kyleellen.net is my artist site.

My contact Kyleellen@me.com

Google Kyleellen or Imagine What's Inside.

More written works are available on Amazon. Music on Spotify, ITunes,

Pandora, etc. Links on Kyleellen.net and email sign up list too.

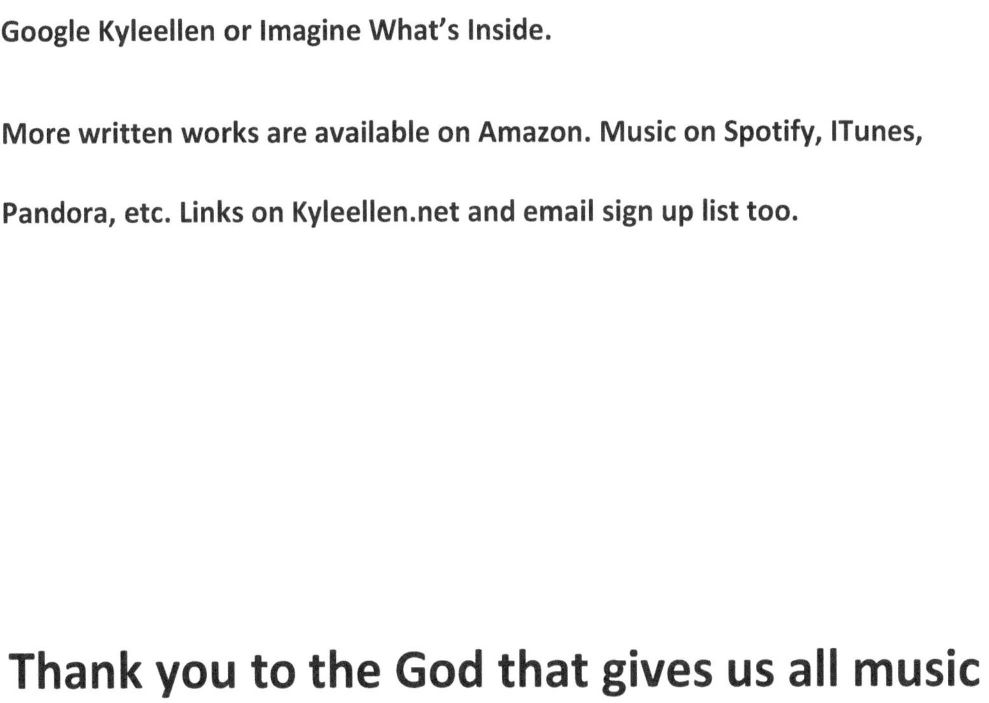

Thank you to the God that gives us all music

and that gave me my passion to sing.